The Secret Government

THE SECRET GOVERNMENT

The Constitution in Crisis

With excerpts from

"An Essay on Watergate"

By Bill Moyers

Introduction by Henry Steele Commager

Seven Locks Press
Cabin John, MD/Washington, DC

Copyright © 1988 by Alvin H. Perlmutter, Inc.,
and Public Affairs Television, Inc.

Library of Congress Cataloging-in-Publication Data

Moyers, Bill D.
    The secret government

"Adapted from two programs of the Public Broadcasting
Service, mainly from one of this same title first broadcast on
November 4, 1987...excerpts from Mr. Moyers' 'Essay on
Watergate,' originally broadcast October 21, 1973" — P.
    Bibliography: p.
    Included index.
    1. Iran-contra Affair, 1985–   . 2. United States.
Central Intelligence Agency.   3. Corruption (in politics)
— United States.   4. Watergate Affair, 1972–1974.
I. Secret government (motion picture)   II. Essay on
Watergate.   III. Title.

E876.M68   1988   973.927   88-3131
ISBN 0-932020-61-5
ISBN 0-932020-60-7   (pbk.)

Manufactured in the United States of America
Designed by Lynn Springer
Typeset by Bets Ltd., Ithaca, N.Y.
Printed by Maple-Vail, York, Pa.

Set in 11-pt. Veljovic and printed on acid-free paper. ∞

    Seven Locks Press
    P.O. Box 27
    Cabin John, MD 20818
    (301) 320-2130

To Joan Konner
and Al Perlmutter
whose love for this
country is no secret.

Credits and Acknowledgments

Photos: Victor Trent, Cover. Robert Llewellyn, p. 14. German Information Service, p. 31. Bill Snead, The Washington Post, p. 50. Michael Springer, p. 70.

Cartoon by Joseph Keppler, p. 62, from *Puck*.

Cartoon by Herblock, p. 63, from *Herblock at Large*. New York: Pantheon Books, 1987. By permission.

The lines from "An Ode in Time of Hesitation" by William Vaughn Moody cited by Dr. Commager can be found in *American Life in Literature*, Jay B. Hubbell, ed. New York: Harper & Brothers, 1936.

Lyrics from "Lives in the Balance" on page 12 © 1986 by Swallow Turn Music, used by permission of the composer, Jackson Browne.

The publisher's special thanks to Tim Justice and Robert P. Hammond, Jr. of the Sony Corporation of America, Lanham, MD., and to Al Levin of Professional Video Transmission Services, Bethesda, MD., for their assistance in converting images from the videotape of "The Secret Government" into black-and-white stills suitable for reproduction in print.

Editor's Note

The Secret Government is adapted from two programs of the Public Broadcasting Service, mainly from one of this same title broadcast on November 4, 1987, the last in Mr. Moyers' series that ran during the bicentennial of the U.S. Constitution. The sections on pages 15–16, 65–84, and 81 are excerpts from Mr. Moyers' "Essay on Watergate," originally broadcast October 21, 1973. Both scripts have been lightly edited, primarily by the elimination of references to television images and by the translation into text of information conveyed graphically in the broadcast versions.

Production, "The Secret Government"

Bill Moyers	Writer, Executive Editor
Alvin H. Perlmutter	Executive Producer
Alan M. Levin	Senior Producer
Paul Budline, Leslie Clark, Marc Levin, Matthew Pook	Producers
Andie Tucher	Editorial Associate
Daphne Pinkerson	Researcher
Jane Murphy Schulberg	Research Consultant
John Farinet, David Houts, Kelly Venardos	Production Assistants
Nancy Pelz-Paget	Project Administration
Douglas P. Sinsel	Production Executive
Joan Konner	Co-Executive Producer

Production, "Essay on Watergate"

Bill Moyers	Writer, Executive Editor
Jerome Toobin	Executive Producer
Martin Clancy	Producer
Jack Sameth	Director

Contents

"Was it for this our fathers kept the law?"

Introduction

HENRY STEELE COMMAGER

The United States today is adding one more chapter to the history of what Barbara Tuchman has called the "March of Folly." Nowhere has this been documented more plainly than in Bill Moyers' television broadcast, "The Secret Government," from which this book is drawn.

Actually, America's record for common sense rather than folly is better than that of most nations. With the exceptions in the nineteenth century of the monomania that drove the South into a four-year war to preserve slavery, and the delusions of empire that led to the acquisition of the Philippines and the "Filipino Insurrection," and — in this century — the dementia that stampeded Congress into a meaningless war in Vietnam, Americans over the years have heeded pretty faithfully Washington's admonition to avoid "permanent, inveterate antipathies against particular nations" and to cultivate "in place of them just and amicable feelings towards all."

Obviously those conducting our foreign policy today no longer heed — indeed, no longer listen to — that farewell address. (At its most recent reading in Congress, the reader addressed an empty hall.) Nor is it likely that they listen to the prophecy of Winston Churchill: "Mankind is now placed in a situation both measureless and laden with doom. Now safety will be the sturdy child of terror, and survival the twin brother of annihi-

HENRY STEELE COMMAGER taught history at Columbia University for almost 20 years before joining the faculty at Amherst College in 1952. He is co-author (with Samuel Eliot Morison) of *The Growth of the American Republic*. Among his best known books on a long list of distinguished works are *The American Mind*, *Living Ideas in America*, and *Freedom, Loyalty, and Dissent*.

lation." No wonder the outlook is bleak. As John Stuart Mill said, "With little men no great things can ever truly be accomplished."

Great things were accomplished by the generation that won independence and wrote the Constitution. Great things were accomplished by the generation that saved the Union and rid it of slavery; by the generation that introduced the New Freedom at home and then went abroad to "save democracy"; and, finally, by a new generation that embraced "general welfare" as essential to "a more perfect union." It was this generation — the generation of Franklin Roosevelt and George Marshall and Averell Harriman — that, when World War II was over, set up the United Nations and the World Court. But, alas, the pendulum had already begun to swing. The shift from Roosevelt to Reagan has some claim to being the most threatening in our history.

The rationalization of the Vietnam War (if that concept is not an oxymoron) and the limitless military buildup that accompanied and succeeded it were natural products of assumptions based on irrelevant premises, not on experience or reality. No better illustration of this than President Nixon's contention that the United States would be a "helpless, crippled giant" if it dared not invade and conquer Cambodia! President Reagan returned to that assumption of American impotence twenty years later when he conjured up the vision of a victorious Nicaragua, backed by that "Empire of Evil," the Soviet Union, confronting the United States along the Rio Grande. This is the kind of rhetoric characterized succinctly by Sen. William Fulbright as one "which robs a nation's policymakers of objectivity and drives them into irresponsible behavior."

There was never any likelihood that Cambodia could defy us; that Vietnam would be able to spread her victory throughout Asia; or, as Secretary Rusk warned us, that China would enter the war and "a million Chinese might land on the shores of

California." But then neither was there much likelihood that the Soviet Union, which suffered some twenty-five million casualties in World War II and whose principal threat has always been China, would somehow launch a military assault upon the United States. Quite aside from any considerations of logic or common sense, the American stockpile of atomic weapons should assuage the fears of both the president and the Pentagon.

If those in high places in Washington were familiar with the history of their own country, they would remember that over a long span of years European monarchies and aristocracies looked upon the United States much as the Nixon and Reagan administrations have looked upon communist countries—with unreasonable fear. Listen to Prince Metternich — in his day the most powerful statesman in Europe — as he fulminates against President Monroe's message of 1823, which we now call the Monroe Doctrine:

> These United States...have suddenly left a sphere too narrow for ambition, and have astonished Europe by a new act of revolt more unprovoked, fully as audacious and no less dangerous than the former. They have announced their intention to set not only power against power, but...altar against altar. In their indecent proclamations they have cast blame and scorn on the institutions of Europe most worthy of respect.... In permitting themselves these unprovoked attacks, in fostering revolutions wherever they show themselves, in extending a helping hand to those which seem to prosper, they lend new strength to the apostles of sedition and re-animate the courage of every conspirator. If this flood of evil doctrines and pernicious exam-

> ples should extend over the whole of America,
> what would become of our political and religious
> institutions, of the moral forces of our govern-
> ment, and of the conservative system which has
> saved Europe from complete dissolution?

Metternich did not call his hostility to the upstart American democracy a "cold war"; neither did he succeed in persuading the Holy Alliance to intervene in American affairs. Yet American democracy and republicanism were incomparably more dangerous to what he and his fellow princes and aristocrats cherished than communism has ever proved to the United States—or is ever likely to prove. Democracy did eventually topple most of the crowned heads of Europe, and equality undermined the class system and — as Metternich predicted — the religious establishment as well. Certainly communism has so far made no significant conquests in the Western Hemisphere. Cuba is scarcely a threat: rather the other way around. The United States somehow managed to deal with the threat from Grenada — if it was a threat — as the award of over eight thousand medals to the invading force of less than eight thousand Marines and Rangers suggests that it must have been.

What communism, specifically Soviet communism, has done is provide us for the first time with the gratification of a national enemy — something that, except by fits and starts, we never really had before in our history. Providence, to be sure, provided us with the Indians, and much of our early folklore dealt with Indian atrocities and American heroism, but the Indian nations never quite assumed the guise of a national enemy. Of course there was England. Tom Paine depicted George III as a despot, but no one could take that seriously. We fought for our independence, and we fought again in 1812, but Andrew Jackson at New Orleans made that war glorious and within a

few years England again was "Our Old Home," and visits to
Stratford-on-Avon and Westminster Abbey obligatory. We fought
what we called a "quasi-war" with France, but France had been
our ally and then Napoleon practically gave us Louisiana — and
there was French food and French fashions to admire. We fought
wars with Mexico and with Spain, and took what we wanted
— Texas, California, Puerto Rico and the Philippines — but our
enmity was short-lived. We fought two wars with Germany and
then, although her crimes were "unforgivable," rebuilt her both
times and made her our ally. We dropped atomic bombs on
Japan, but made her our ally, too, and our protégé until she
became our economic rival. We never went to war with Russia.
Indeed, she had supported the American War for Independence
and sided with the Union during the Civil War and practically
gave us Alaska; and how much longer might World War II have
lasted if it were not for the Soviet Union siding with the Allied
powers? But then it was not the Soviet Union alone that became
our national enemy, but rather communism — an enemy easy
to conjure up and to hate. Fear of communism, hatred of the
national enemy, united all parties, all religions, and above all,
all interests. And so the cold war deepened and spread from
Europe to Asia to Cuba and Nicaragua, but the identification
of the national enemy changed from a communism in general
to be combatted globally, to the Soviet Union in particular. We
do not fight communists in Cuba or in Nicaragua but agents
of the Soviet Union! We do not declare war on those countries,
but we send mercenaries against them because we are warring
somewhat inconclusively on the Soviet Union.

Corruption reveals itself first in language. So Thucydides said
in his memorable paragraph on the extravagance of revolutionary zeal:

> What used to be described as a thoughtless act
> of aggression was now regarded as the courage

> one would expect to find in a party member; to
> think of the future was merely one way of saying
> one was a coward. Fanatical enthusiasm was the
> mark of a real man. . . . Anyone who held violent
> opinions could always be trusted and. . .to plot
> successfully was a sign of intelligence.

Corruption of language is a special form of deception that recent administrations and the Pentagon have brought to a high degree of perfection. Bombing is "protective reaction"; precision bombing is "surgical strikes"; guerrilla insurgents are "freedom fighters." What would we have thought had Britain designated the Confederates of 1861 as "freedom fighters"? Even Orwell's *1984* does not imagine a doublethink as deceptive as that which now emanates from Washington.

Along with the corruption of language goes, of course, the corruption of truth. If there were lies during the Vietnam years — and lies there were — nothing can compare with the corruption of truth of the Reagan administration. As Mr. Moyers writes, "The administration pursued a policy of secrecy shrouded in lies, and of passion cloaked in fiction." Indeed, where totalitarian regimes invented the Big Lie, it has remained for the Reagan administration to develop a more effective device: that of lies so innumerable, and so preposterous, that no one could keep up with them, so insolent that they confounded even those who invented them, and so shameless that they benumbed the moral sensibilities of their sponsors.

All of this has been attended and justified by claims of moral superiority. After all, if our hearts are pure, our intentions honorable, and our motives disinterested, what we do — however it might look to the uninitiated — should not be judged by the standards that history applies to the misdeeds and corruptions of other nations. Claims of moral superiority for the United

States did not originate with Ronald Reagan's staff. What the poet William Vaughn Moody wrote in his anguished protest of our war against the Filipinos struggling for independence must be said of our conduct in Vietnam and Cuba, and of our conduct in Nicaragua today:

> Lies! Lies! It cannot be! The wars we wage
> Are noble, and our battles still are won
> By justice for us, ere we lift the gage.
> We have not sold our loftiest heritage.
> The proud republic hath not stooped to cheat
> And scramble in the market-place of war;
> Her forehead weareth yet its solemn star. . . .
>
> Was it for this our fathers kept the law?

*   *   *

Bill Moyers is primarily a reporter and an essayist, a craftsman and an artist working in a medium that has proven generally inhospitable to thoughtful documentary and to anything that can't be said in twenty-second "bites." In some of his work for television—especially in the summaries with which he customarily closes his broadcasts—there is often a challenging lyricism close to the poetry of William Vaughn Moody. Moyers is like Moody, too, in that he speaks from conscience, out of an intelligent patriotism and with a sure sense of what America is all about. And just as in an earlier period of national crisis Moody asked us to consider seriously our history and our prophecy, so does Moyers today in "The Secret Government."

Amherst, Massachusetts
March, 1988

The Secret Government

LT. COL. OLIVER NORTH:

And I still, to this day, Counsel, don't see anything wrong with taking the Ayatollah's money and sending it to support the Nicaraguan freedom fighters.

GEORGE GORMAN:

They have basically said to the entire United States, "We don't care what the people say, we don't care what the Congress says, we don't care what the other oversight organizations say. We're going to find some way to rid the planet of communism, and we don't care who gets killed in the process."

PRES. RONALD REAGAN:

As long as there is breath in this body, I will speak and work, strive and struggle, for the cause of the Nicaraguan freedom fighters.

COL. PHILIP ROETTINGER:
Freedom fighters they are
not. They are terrorists.

SCOTT ARMSTRONG:
Wait a minute. This isn't the
way the Constitution was set
up. This isn't what the
Founding Fathers intended.

MORTON HALPERIN:

You start out breaking foreign laws since most countries have laws against
secretly overthrowing their
governments, and then you
end up breaking the law at
home.

FAWN HALL:

Sometimes you have to go above the written law.

SEN. JOHN KERRY:

They were willing to literally put the Constitution at risk because they believed somehow there was a higher order of things.

WOMAN:

We have liberty, and the only way we're going to keep liberty is to have people who are strong, like Reagan and North.

VIETNAM VETERAN:

Violence is not the answer.
You don't teach the
democratic way by shoving
an M-16 down somebody's
throat.

ROGER WILKINS:

If we continue these policies, to rob ourselves in order to feed this national
security monster, we are going to continue to degrade
American life.

NANCY JONES:

We're only talking about subverting the Constitution, that's all.

Although the 200th anniversary of our Constitution is behind us, we continue to debate the document's meaning. It's a debate that news events renew almost daily. It's about war and peace, freedom and justice. It's heard from the Capitol down to Main Street, and in this song by pop star Jackson Browne:

> I've been waiting for something to happen
> For a week or a month or a year,
> With the blood in the ink of the headlines
> And the sound of the crowd in my ear..
> You might ask what it takes to remember
> When you know that you've seen it before
> Where a government lies to a people
> And a country is drifting to war.
>
> There's a shadow on the faces
> Of the men who send the guns
> To the wars that are fought in places
> Where their business interest runs.
>
> On the radio talk shows and the TV
> You'll hear one thing again and again:
> How the U.S.A. stands for freedom
> And we've come to the aid of a friend.
> But who are the ones that we call our friends?
> These governments killing their own?
> Or the people who finally can't take any more
> And they pick up a gun or a brick or a stone?

I'm Bill Moyers. In this
essay, we'll look at that
government in the shadows.

"The Enterprise" 1.

I first came to the nation's capital in 1954 — more than 34 years ago — to work as a summer intern on the staff of Senate Majority Leader Lyndon Johnson. On my first weekend, I climbed to the top of the Washington Monument and looked down on the temples of our national faith. First, the White House. Every president except George Washington slept here. In grade school I had never been able to remember the name of Millard Fillmore when the teacher asked us to list the presidents in order, but during this first summer in Washington even Fillmore's portrait evoked images of Titans. Then, across the Tidal Basin, to the memorial to Thomas Jefferson. "The whole of government," Jefferson wrote, "consists in the art of being honest." Next I shifted my vision to the pensive figure of Abraham Lincoln — brooding, it seemed to me, over the unknown destiny of the Union for whose survival he had become a martyr. And, finally, the Capitol. A teacher in high school used to tell us, "There is no sight more beautiful in the world than a people governing." The first time I saw the Capitol dome, I remembered what she said and got a lump in my throat. On the steps of the Capitol's eastern portico, every president since Monroe has received his oath of office; 34 years ago, fresh out of Texas, I thought that all of them had to be giants, that somehow the office made them larger than life.

It was all so intoxicating to a schoolboy who had never been east of the Red River that I would make this same round almost every Sunday, starting early in the morning and seldom getting back before twilight to the room I rented on Capitol Hill. Like so many of my generation I had come out of school with a one-sided view of American history. To this day, I remember one teacher insisting that "in the 5,000 years of the human race, there has never been a more principled, moral or virtuous nation than the United States of America." He believed it, and we believed him. The books and legends told a romantic tale of selfless people in the service of God and nation. Where I grew up, the Almighty and Uncle Sam were inseparable, and the preacher on Sunday seldom failed to remind us that we Americans were the Chosen People — because we deserved to be. We were great because we were good, and if we remained good, we would remain great. We were taught to look on government as a blessing and to respect authority for its own sake. The splendid monuments with their noble inscriptions merely confirmed the altruism we had been taught to believe was the essence of the American experience.

But for 40 years a secret government has been growing behind these stately tributes to American ideals, growing like a cancer on the Constitution.

It's what people were talking about during the summer of 1987: the abuse of power, a breach of faith. I interviewed some at random:

> FIRST MAN: Not everybody tells the truth. Not everybody thinks that the public is entitled to know the truth. And not everybody thinks they should go by the law.

WOMAN: But I don't think we'll ever know the truth about what really happened. I mean, I feel like there are still lies out there and we still don't know.

SECOND MAN: The thing that I started thinking was, this must happen all the time; this time they just got caught.

People lined up early every day to listen in person to the Iran-contra hearings, while millions watched on television. Members of the secret government had been forced from the shadows into the spotlight.

LT. COL. OLIVER NORTH (Iran-contra hearings): I will tell you right now, Counsel, and all the members here gathered, that I misled the Congress.

JOHN NIELDS, House chief counsel: At that meeting?

COLONEL NORTH: At that meeting.

MR. NIELDS: Face to face?

COLONEL NORTH: Face to face.

MR. NIELDS: You made false statements to them about your activities in support of the contras?

COLONEL NORTH: I did.

Oliver North had been the secret government's chronic liar, long on zeal for his president and the cause. He was not the only zealot, not the only one to deceive. The hearings revealed a wholesale policy of secrecy shrouded in lies, of passion cloaked in fiction and deception. But the hearings told only part of the story, so let's begin on Day One.

> PRESIDENT REAGAN (January 1981): I, Ronald
> Reagan, do solemnly swear. . . .

Reagan came to office promising to restore America's military and moral prestige in the world. Voters had responded when he pledged to be tough on terrorists, a vow he repeated time and again.

> PRESIDENT REAGAN: Let me further make it plain
> to the assassins in Beirut and their accomplices,
> wherever they may be, that America will never
> make concessions to terrorists.

That's what the president kept saying, but it's not what he was doing. The story broke on November 3, 1986, in a magazine in Lebanon: the United States had defied its own embargo on arms to Iran. Ronald Reagan was offering weapons to the Ayatollah Khomeini in return for the release of American hostages. The president went on television to deny it.

> PRESIDENT REAGAN (November 13, 1986):
> The charge has been made that the United States
> has shipped weapons to Iran as ransom payment
> for the release of American hostages in Lebanon,
> that the United States undercut its allies and

secretly violated American policy against traffick-
ing with terrorists. Those charges are utterly false.

The president was not telling the truth. And when he held a
news conference the next week, the pattern of deception
continued.

REPORTER (November 19, 1986): Mr. President, I
don't think it's still clear just what Israel's role
was in this. Could you explain what the Israeli
role was here?

PRESIDENT REAGAN: No, because we, as I say,
have had nothing to do with other countries or
their shipment of arms, or doing what they're —
they are doing.

That wasn't the truth either. Half an hour later, the White House
press office corrected the president: Israel had been a key player
in the sale of arms to Iran. Rapidly now, the web of secrets was
unraveling. On November 25, the president's old friend and ally,
Atty. Gen. Edwin Meese, revealed the deepest secret of all.

ATTORNEY GENERAL MEESE (November 25, 1986):
Certain moneys, which were received in the trans-
action between representatives of Israel and
representatives of Iran, were taken and made
available to the forces in Central America [that]
are opposing the Sandinista government there.

The Constitution is ambiguous on many things, but not on this.
The president "shall take care that the laws be faithfully executed." Yet Reagan himself approved selling arms to Iran, and as

for the illegal diversion of funds to the contras — well, the president's former national security adviser said the decision had been his.

> ADM. JOHN POINDEXTER (Iran-contra hearings): I made a very deliberate decision not to ask the president, so that I could insulate him from the decision and provide some future deniability for the president if it ever leaked out.

But there was no denying that the president's men knew what was in the president's mind.

> ADMIRAL POINDEXTER: And he had been very adamant at the time, that he says, "Look, I don't want to pull out our support for the contras for any reason. This would be an unacceptable option. Isn't there something that I could do unilaterally?"

"Unilaterally." In other words, without congressional approval. Ronald Reagan's message was clear: find some way, any way, to help the contras.

> PRESIDENT REAGAN: So I guess in a way they are counter revolutionary, and God bless them for being that way. And I guess that makes them contras, and so it makes me a contra too.

The contras: Reagan has compared them to our Founding Fathers. In reality, Ronald Reagan and CIA director William Casey were *their* founding fathers. Two months after his inauguration, the president approved the funds Casey used to create the contras. Their ultimate goal was the violent overthrow of the Nicaraguan government, a government the United States legally recognizes. So the war had to be carried out covertly, as a campaign of terror. But Americans were outraged when CIA agents mined the Nicaraguan harbors and blew up fuel tanks, causing thousands of Nicaraguan citizens to flee their homes; and Congress, in protest, cut off the contra funds. Still the president refused to give up on his crusade, and his men went to work secretly to keep the war going. The question now was how to evade Congress, the law and public opinion.

First, a small cabal in the White House took charge of policy: President Reagan, CIA Director Casey, National Security Advisers McFarlane and Poindexter, and their aide, Colonel North.

To raise money for the contras, the secret team turned to right-wing governments that could do favors for the United States and receive favors in return. The king of Saudi Arabia doled out a million dollars a month; the sultan of Brunei coughed up $10 million that was misplaced through a White House error. The secret government also encouraged the fund-raising efforts of retired Gen. John Singlaub. Relieved of his command for insubordination in 1977, he now runs the World Anti-Communist League.

> GEN. JOHN SINGLAUB (speaking to contras):
> I represent hundreds of thousands of Americans
> who are sympathetic to your cause and want to
> help.

Here at home, wealthy right-wingers were solicited directly by North. Some of them were told their contributions would get them invited to the Oval Office. Conservative activist Carl Channell, who later pleaded guilty to conspiracy to defraud the government, worked directly with Colonel North, pumping donors like investor Joseph O'Boyle.

> SEN. PAUL SARBANES, D-Md. (Iran-contra hearings):
> I take it your encounters involved — invariably involved — both Mr. Channell and Colonel North. And maybe Channell took you to North and then you met with North and then subsequently you would meet with Channell. But in a sense, they worked as a team.

> MR. O'BOYLE: In a sense, yes.

> SENATOR SARBANES: Mrs. Garwood, is that true in your instance, as well?

> ELLEN GARWOOD:* I would say that's a fairly accurate description.

All this was being done to advance the president's policies, but it wasn't enough. To get around the law, the White House then enlisted the services of something called "The Enterprise."

> GEN. RICHARD V. SECORD (Iran-contra hearings):
> The Enterprise is the group of companies that Mr.

---

* Ellen Clayton Garwood is identified in the *Report of the Congressional Committees Investigating the Iran-Contra Affair* as "a wealthy octogenarian widow from a well-known family in Austin, Texas." All told, she contributed $2,515,135 in 1986 to the National Endowment for the Preservation of Liberty, Carl Channell's tax-exempt fund-raising organization. Ms. Garwood testified that these contributions were mainly for the purchase of weapons and ammunition chosen from a list provided by Channell and North.

Hakim formed to manage the contra and the
Iranian project.

ARTHUR LIMAN, Senate chief counsel: Who controls
the Enterprise?

GENERAL SECORD: I exercised overall control.

Gen. Richard Secord, now retired, has been in and out of covert
operations for a quarter-century. One of the first Americans to
fly secret missions in Vietnam, he also helped run the CIA's
secret war in Laos. Secord became a major Pentagon figure in
foreign military sales, especially to the Shah of Iran. That's where
he met Albert Hakim.

MR. HAKIM (Iran-contra hearings): Not only was I
presented with an opportunity to help my country, the United States, and my native land, Iran,
but at the same time I had the opportunity to
profit financially.

Hakim was Secord's partner in the Enterprise. Born in Iran, he
made millions selling American-made arms to the shah, often
relying on bribes and illegal payoffs to ease the way. Now he
handled financial matters for the Enterprise. Like any good business, the Enterprise was designed to make money.

MR. LIMAN (Iran-contra hearings): Am I correct, Mr.
Secord, that from December 1984 until July 1985,
you were engaged in selling arms to the contras
for profit?

GENERAL SECORD: That's correct.

Then, at the direct request of the secret White House team, the Enterprise brokered American arms to the Ayatollah Khomeini. Beyond Secord and Hakim, it grew to include a shadowy network of arms dealers, fraudulent companies, and secret bank accounts. The Enterprise was, as Sen. Daniel Inouye (D-Hawaii) put it, "a shadowy government with its own air force, its own navy, its own fund-raising mechanism, and the ability to pursue its own ideas of the national interest, free from all checks and balances and free from the law itself."

Here's just one example of how the Enterprise worked. With the full knowledge of William Casey and Oliver North, Secord and Hakim controlled secret bank accounts in Switzerland that received those contributions from private citizens. The money was then funneled to the contras. One donor was Joseph Coors, the millionaire beer tycoon. Coors met directly with Casey, who referred him to North.

> MR. COORS (Iran-contra hearings): I told him that I was interested in — in seeing what I could do, and I asked him for his recommendations.
>
> JAMIE KAPLAN, Senate assistant counsel: And did North subsequent to the meeting provide you the Swiss bank account name and number to which your payments should be made?
>
> MR. COORS: Yes, he did.

Joseph Coors deposited $65,000 into the secret account, but that was peanuts compared to the arms deals. Secord purchased a thousand missiles from the CIA for $3.7 million and sold them to an Iranian middleman for $10 million. On that one transaction alone, after expenses, the Enterprise made a profit of $5.5

million, almost 200 percent. Its overall profits on the sales to Iran may have been as much as $15 million.

> REP. JIM COURTER, R-N.J. (Iran-contra hearings): You did, in fact, use some of those proceeds, approximately — and correct me if my recollection is wrong — about $3.5 million for the contra effort in Central America?

> GENERAL SECORD: Yes, sir.

But most of the money never reached the contras, including $8 million dollars that as far as we know remains in a private Swiss account. Operating in secret, the Enterprise was free to put profits above patriotism. They even sold arms directly to the contras at a huge markup.

> SENATOR SARBANES (Iran-contra hearings): If the purpose of the Enterprise was to help the contras, why did you charge Calero a markup that included a profit?

> GENERAL SECORD: We were in business to make a living, Senator. We had to make — we had to make a living. I didn't see anything wrong with it at the time; it was a commercial enterprise.

> SENATOR SARBANES: Oh, I thought the purpose of the Enterprise was to — was to aid Calero's cause.

> GENERAL SECORD: Can't I have two purposes? I did.

While profits were being made, lives were being lost. Iran has used missiles supplied by the Enterprise to fight its war against

Iraq. That war has already lasted more than seven years, leaving as many as a million people killed or wounded.

And in Nicaragua the contras use weapons from the Enterprise against civilians. It's a terrorist war they're fighting; innocent men, women, and children are caught in the middle or killed deliberately as the contras use violence against peasants to pressure their government. Thousands have died. Even as the hearings were taking place in Washington during the summer of 1987, a contra raid in Nicaragua killed three children and a pregnant woman.

The casualties mounted while the secret government in Washington knew that the contra leaders were not such noble freedom fighters, after all. Colonel North learned that from his own liaison with the contras, Robert Owen.

> MR. OWEN (Iran-contra hearings): I was but a private foot soldier who believed in the cause of the Nicaraguan democratic resistance.

Owen sent a secret memo to his boss, reminding North that the chief contra leader, Adolfo Calero, is a creation of the U.S. government and warning him that those around Calero "are not first-rate people. They're liars, greed- and power-motivated. This war has become a business to many of them." Owen's judgment has been supported by disillusioned rebels who quit the struggle in disgust with contra leaders.

> ALBERTO SUHR, former contra officer: People who have never dirtied their boots, people who never went to the field, people who didn't even know how to pick up a rifle, pretending, being a façade for the CIA, and whose only concern was making

money. They bought shoddy goods and put them
at hiked-up prices. They bought low-grade grains
like rice and beans and corn and sugar and salt,
and put them up for sale or billed them to themselves at the highest prices. They did the same
with ammunitions; they did the same with rifles.

The contempt for Congress, the defiance of law, the huge mark-
ups and profits, the secret bank accounts, the shady characters, the shakedown of foreign governments, the complicity in
death and destruction — they did all this in the dark because
it would never stand the light of day. Secrecy is the freedom
zealots dream of: no watchman to check the door, no accountant to check the books, no judge to check the law. The secret
government has no constitution. The rules it follows are the
rules it makes up. So William Casey could dream that the Enterprise might take on a life of its own, permanent and wholly
unaccountable.

COLONEL NORTH (Iran-contra hearings):
The director was interested in the ability to go to
an existing, as he put it, off-the-shelf, self-
sustaining, stand-alone entity that could perform
certain activities on behalf of the United States.

MR. LIMAN: Are you not shocked that the director
of Central Intelligence is proposing to you the creation of an organization to do these kinds of
things, outside of his own organization?

COLONEL NORTH: Counsel, I can tell you I'm not
shocked.

Sen. John Kerry, a veteran of the Vietnam war, is a member of the Senate Foreign Relations Committee.

> SEN. JOHN KERRY, D-Mass.: They were willing to literally put the Constitution at risk because they believed somehow there was a higher order of things, that the ends do in fact justify, are justified by, the means. That's the most Marxist, totalitarian doctrine I've ever heard of in my life. If you can have a retired general and a colonel, you know, in mufti, running around, making deals in other countries on their own, soliciting funds to wage wars to overthrow governments, and hide it from the American people so you have no accountability, you've done the very thing that James Madison and others feared most when they were struggling to put the Constitution together, which was to create an accountable system which didn't have runaway power, which didn't concentrate power in one hand so that you could have one person making a decision and running off against the will of the American people.

What could possibly justify it? The fight against communism, of course.

> COLONEL NORTH (Iran-contra hearings):
> This nation cannot abide the communization of Central America. We cannot have Soviet bases on the mainland of this hemisphere.

It means dirty wars and dirty tricks, lying and deceit.

MR. NIELDS (Iran-contra hearings): These operations were designed to be secrets from the American people.

COLONEL NORTH: Mr. Nields, I am at a loss as to how we could announce it to the American people and not have the Soviets know about it.

MR. NIELDS: Well, in fact, Colonel North, you believed that the Soviets were aware of our sale of arms to Iran, weren't you?

COLONEL NORTH: It — we came to a point in time when we were concerned about that.

Since our adversaries know about covert operations, the only people fooled are the American people. But consent is the very heart of our constitutional system. How can people judge what they do not know, or what they are told falsely?

MR. NIELDS (Iran-contra hearings): We do live in a democracy, don't we?

COLONEL NORTH: We do, sir, thank God.

MR. NIELDS: In which it is the people, not one Marine lieutenant colonel, that get to decide the important policy decisions for the nation.

COLONEL NORTH: Yes.

It isn't the first time that men who express reverence for democracy in public have violated the values of democracy in practice. The secret government is an interlocking network of official functionaries, spies, mercenaries, ex-generals, profiteers, and superpatriots, who for a variety of motives operate outside the legitimate institutions of government. Presidents have turned to them when they can't win the support of Congress or the people, exercising that unsupervised power so feared by the framers of our Constitution.

Imagine that William Casey's dream came true. Suppose the Enterprise grew into a supersecret, self-financing, self-perpetuating organization. Suppose its operators decided on their own to assassinate Gorbachev or the leader of white South Africa. Could a president control them? And what if he became the Enterprise's Public Enemy Number One? Who would know? Who would say no?

During the Bolshevik revolution in Russia, Lenin created the *Cheka*, a secret organization run by eight lieutenants reporting directly to him and filled with zealots who terrorized opponents. They made up their own rules, they chose their own missions, and they judged their own operations. You say it can't happen here? Well, before deciding for sure, let's look at the history of our secret government.

2.
The Cold,
Cold
Warriors

Berlin Wall, 1965

The
Cold, Cold
Warriors   2.

World War II was over. Europe lay devastated. The United States emerged as the most powerful nation on earth. But from the rubble rose a strange new world: a peace that was not peace and a war that was not war. We saw it emerging when the Soviets occupied Eastern Europe.

> WINSTON CHURCHILL (Fulton, Mo., March 5, 1946):
> An iron curtain has descended across the continent. Behind that line lie all the capitals of the ancient states of Central and Eastern Europe.

The cold war had begun. The Russians had been our ally against the Nazis, an expedient alliance for the sake of war. Now they were our enemy. To fight them we turned to some of the very men who had inflicted on humanity the horrors of Hitler's madness.

We hired Nazis as American spies. We struck a secret bargain with the devil.

ERHARD DABRINGHAUS, former counterintelligence
agent: One that I know real well is Klaus Barbie.
He was wanted by the French as their number-
one war criminal. And somehow we employed a
man like that as a very secretive informant.

Dabringhaus was employed in the U.S. Army Counter-
Intelligence Corps and assigned to work with Nazi informants
spying on the Russians. One of the them was Klaus Barbie, the
Butcher of Lyons, who had tortured and murdered thousands
of Jews and resistance fighters.

MR. DABRINGHAUS: During the time I learned
that Barbie was really such a brutal murderer, I
reported this to my headquarters and I thought I
was going to get a promotion. I thought that was
a big picture of a deal I had here, you know. And
the answer was "Dabringhaus, keep quiet until
he's no longer useful; then we'll turn him over to
the French." Under those conditions, I thought,
well, okay, let's work with him, you know. If
you're an intelligence officer, you work with the
devil.

The Americans did not turn Barbie over to the French when
they finished with him. They helped him escape to Bolivia.
Other top Nazis were smuggled into the United States, to cooperate in the war against the new enemy. Dabringhaus still remem-
bers the attitude of his superiors: the new enemy was the only
enemy.

MR. DABRINGHAUS: They seemed to have had a
preconceived program of what the communists

are up to, and if I sent in a report that there was
a Nazi war criminal running around over there,
"Forget it, we're not interested in the Nazis any-
more; we're concentrating on the communists."

So began the morality of the cold war: anything goes. The struggle required a mentality of permanent war, a perpetual state
of emergency, and it meant a vast new apparatus of power that
radically transformed our government. Its foundations were laid
when President Truman signed into law the National Security
Act of 1947.

> ADM. GENE LAROCQUE: Now that National Security
> Act of 1947 changed dramatically the direction of
> this great nation. It established the framework for
> a national security state.

Retired Admiral LaRocque rose through the ranks from ensign
to become a strategic planner for the Pentagon. He now heads
the Center for Defense Information, a public interest group.

> ADMIRAL LAROCQUE: The National Security Act
> of '47 gave us the National Security Council.
> Never have we had a national security council so
> concerned about the nation's security that we
> were always looking for threats and looking how
> to orchestrate our society to oppose those threats.
> National security was invented almost in 1947,
> and now it has become the prime mover of every-
> thing we do, is measured against something we
> invented in 1947. The National Security Act also
> gave us the Central Intelligence Agency.

The CIA became the core of the new secret government. Its chief legitimate duty was to gather foreign intelligence for America's role as a world power. Soon it was taking on covert operations abroad and at home. As its mission expanded, the agency recruited adventuresome young men like Notre Dame's all-American Ralph McGehee.

> MR. MCGEHEE, former CIA agent: I look back to the individual that I was when I joined the agency. I was a dedicated Cold Warrior, who felt the agency was out there fighting for liberty, justice, democracy, and religion around the world. And I believed wholeheartedly in this. I just felt proud every day that I went to work because I was out at the vanguard of the battle against the international evil empire, international communist evil empire.

Iran, 1953. The CIA mounted its first major covert operation to overthrow a foreign government. The target was the prime minister of Iran, Mohammed Mossadegh. He held power legitimately through his country's parliamentary process. Washington had once looked to him as the man to prevent a communist takeover. But that was before Mossadegh decided that the Iranian state, not British companies, ought to own and control the oil within Iran's own borders. When he nationalized the British-run oil fields, Washington saw red. Kennett Love was a young New York Times reporter in Teheran that summer.

> MR. LOVE: This was in McCarthy's time,* and the whole cold war paranoia was running wild in

---

*See page 75n, McCarthy

Washington. And everybody was saying that crazy
old Mossadegh was falling under the influence of
the communists. This was not true.

MANSOUR FARHANG, writer: He did not receive an
iota of assistance from the Soviet Union.

Mansour Farhang was a young student activist in Teheran and
a Mossadegh supporter. He now lives in the United States as
a teacher and a writer.

MR. FARHANG: In those days, in the early '50s,
the idea of an independent, neutral state was not
at all acceptable to either the West, either the
United States or the Soviet Union. Mossadegh was
a victim of this East-West rivalry.

The secretary of state, John Foster Dulles, and his brother Allen,
director of the CIA, decided with Eisenhower's approval to overthrow Mossadegh and reinstate the Shah of Iran. Love recalls
the work of one American agent, George Carroll.

MR. LOVE: He was the one that paid the money
to the street gangs. He was the one that invented
the idea to make everybody identify himself as
the shah's partisan, so therefore the opposition
would not be able to group in the streets. That
was why everybody in a vehicle and anything else
had to put a shah's picture in the windshield and
put the headlights on. You had to or you would
have your windshield clubbed in and be dragged
out and beaten up and killed or whatever.

The mobs paid by the CIA, and the police and soldiers bribed by the CIA, drove Mossadegh from office.

> NEWSREEL ANNOUNCER (August 1953): Crown
> Prince Abdullah greets the shah as he lands at
> Baghdad Airport after a seven-hour flight from
> Rome.

The King of Kings was back in control and more pliable than Mossadegh. American oil companies took over almost half of Iran's production. U.S. arms merchants moved in with $18 billion of weapons sales over the next 20 years. But there were losers.

> MR. LOVE: Nearly everybody in Iran of any impor-
> tance has had a brother or a mother or a sister or
> a son or a father tortured, jailed, deprived of
> property without due process. I mean, an abso-
> lutely buccaneering dictatorship in our name, that
> we supported. SAVAK was created by the CIA.

SAVAK, the shah's secret police, tortured and murdered thousands of his opponents. Gen. Richard Secord and Albert Hakim were among those who helped supply the shah's insatiable appetite for the technology of control.

But the weapons and flattery America heaped on the shah blinded us to the growing opposition of his own people. They rose up in 1979 against him. "Death to the shah," they shouted, "Death to the American Satan."

> MR. LOVE: Khomeini is a direct consequence, and
> the hostage crisis is a direct consequence, and the

resurgence of the shah is a direct consequence of the CIA's overthrow of Mossadegh in 1953.

EDWIN FIRMAGE, University of Utah: It's cited often as a wonderful example of an efficient CIA accomplishing something good. In reality —

Firmage is a professor of law, a former White House Fellow, and a constitutional scholar.

PROFESSOR FIRMAGE: You create a nation who hates you enormously, who views you as a devil, an evil force. You create in that state sufficient forces of unrest that you don't have stability. And those — those chickens come home to roost; you end up with a violation of the Constitution and a hatred that is propagated today, until you have embassies taken, hostages held, hatred engendered. Hatred simply doesn't come to rest.

Guatemala, 1954. Flushed with success, America's secret government decided another troublesome leader must go. This time it was Jacobo Arbenz, the democratically elected president of Guatemala. Col. Philip Roettinger, now retired, was recruited from the Marines to join the CIA team.

COLONEL ROETTINGER: It was explained to me that it was very important for the security of the United States, that we were going to prevent a Soviet beachhead in this hemisphere — which we have heard about very recently, of course — and that the Guatemalan government was communist and we had to do something about it.

President Arbenz was no paragon of virtue, but he had admired Franklin Delano Roosevelt and his government voted often with the American position at the United Nations. He was the head of a government that, in fact, committed no act against the United States. But he did commit two sins in the eyes of the Eisenhower administration. First, when he opened the system to all political parties, he recognized the communists, too.

> COLONEL ROETTINGER: Well, of course, there was no — not even a hint of communism in his government. He had no communists in his cabinet; he did permit the existence of a very small communist party.

Arbenz also embarked on a massive land reform program. Less than 3 percent of the landowners held more than 70 percent of the land. Arbenz nationalized more than 1.5 million acres, including land owned by his own family, and turned it over to peasants. Much of that land belonged to the United Fruit Co., the giant American firm that was intent on keeping Guatemala quite literally a banana republic. United Fruit appealed to its close friends in Washington, including the Dulles brothers, who said that Arbenz was openly playing the communist game. He had to go.

> COLONEL ROETTINGER: This was sudden death for him. I mean, there was no chance of him winning this fight because he had done this to the United Fruit Co. Plus the fact that he was overthrowing the hegemony of the United States over this area, and this was dangerous. It could not be tolerated. We couldn't tolerate this.

From Honduras, the same country that today is the contra staging base, the CIA launched a small band of mercenaries against Guatemala. They were easily turned back. Then, with its own planes and pilots, the CIA bombed the capital. Arbenz fled and was immediately replaced by an American puppet, Col. Carlos Castillo Armas.

> COLONEL ROETTINGER: He overturned all of the reformist activity of President Arbenz. He gave the land back to the United Fruit Co. that had been confiscated; he took land from the peasants and gave it back to the landowners.

The CIA had called its covert action against Guatemala "Operation Success." Military dictators ruled the country for the next 30 years. The United States provided them with weapons and trained their officers. The communists we saved them from would have been hard-pressed to do it better. Peasants were slaughtered, political opponents were tortured, suspected insurgents were shot, stabbed, burned alive, or strangled. There were so many deaths at one point that coroners complained they couldn't keep up with the workload. "Operation Success."

> COLONEL ROETTINGER: What we did has caused a succession of repressive military dictatorships in that country and has been responsible for the death of over 100,000 of their citizens.

Success breeds success, sometimes with dreary repetition. Mario Sandoval Alarcon began his career in the CIA's adventure in Guatemala. Today he's known as a godfather of the death squads. In 1981, after lobbying Reagan's advisers for military aid to Guatemala, Sandoval danced at the inaugural ball.

Richard Bissell, another veteran of the Guatemalan coup, went on to become the CIA's chief of covert operations. I looked him up several years ago for a CBS documentary. He talked about a secret report prepared for the White House in 1954 by a group of distinguished citizens headed by former president Herbert Hoover. That report read, in part: "It is now clear that we are facing an implacable enemy whose avowed objective is world domination.... There are no rules in such a game. Hitherto accepted norms of human conduct do not apply.... If the United States is to survive, long-standing American concepts of fair play must be reconsidered.... We must learn to subvert, sabotage and destroy our enemies by more clever, more sophisticated, more effective methods than those used against us." In my 1977 interview with Mr. Bissell, I asked him if this conclusion of the Hoover Report represented the prevailing ethic.

> MR. BISSELL: I think that's an excellent statement of the prevailing view, at least the view of those who'd had any contact with covert operations of one kind or another.

> MOYERS: In other words, the nature of the enemy is such that any tactics are necessary, are justified, in order to thwart him and defeat him?"

> MR. BISSELL: I believe that was the view. It certainly was my view at the time.

Cuba, 1961. Seven years after Operation Success in Guatemala, Bissell was planning another CIA covert operation.

> NEWSREEL ANNOUNCER: The assault has begun on the dictatorship of Fidel Castro.

On April 17, 1961, Cuban exiles trained by the CIA at a base in friendly Guatemala landed on the southern coast of Cuba, at the Bay of Pigs. The United States had promised air support, but Pres. John F. Kennedy canceled it. Left defenseless, the invaders surrendered.

Seven months after the disastrous invasion, Kennedy delivered a major foreign policy address.

> PRESIDENT KENNEDY (November 1961): We cannot as a free nation compete with our adversaries in tactics of terror, assassination, false promises, counterfeit mobs, and crises.

The president was not telling the truth. Even as he spoke, his administration was planning a new covert war on Cuba. It would include some of the dirty tricks the president said we were above. The secret government was prepared for anything. I recall asking Mr. Bissell:

> MOYERS: At one time, the CIA organized a small department known as "executive action," which was a permanent assassination capability. How did that — ?

> MR. BISSELL: Well, it wasn't just an assassination capability, it was a capability to discredit or get rid of people. But it could have included assassination.

And it did. There were at least eight documented attempts to kill Castro. He says there were two dozen. And there was even one effort to put LSD in his cigars. To help us get rid of the Cuban leader, our secret government turned to the Mafia, as we once

made use of Nazis. The gangsters included the Las Vegas mafi-
oso John Roselli; the don of Chicago, Sam Giancana; and the
boss of Tampa, Santo Trafficante.

> MR. BISSELL: I think we should not have involved
> ourselves with the Mafia. I think an organization
> that does so is losing control of the security of its
> information. I think we should have been afraid
> that we would open ourselves to blackmail.

> MOYERS: If I read you correctly, you're saying it's
> the involvement with the Mafia that disturbed you
> and not the need or decision to assassinate a
> foreign leader.

> MR. BISSELL: Correct.

It's a chilling thought, made more chilling by the assassination
of John Kennedy. The accusations linger; the suspicions per-
sist of a dark, unsolved conspiracy behind his murder. You can
dismiss them, as many of us do, but since we know now what
our secret government planned for Castro, the possibility remains: once we decide that anything goes, anything can come
home to haunt us.

> REP. JIM LEACH, R-Iowa: The sad thing of the last
> few years — both with regard to Central America,
> where our covert activities have included assassi-
> nation manuals, as well as what may have oc-
> curred in Libya with regard to a bombing raid on
> Qaddafi, a person no American can sympathize
> with — is that the assassination issue has reared
> its head again as an extreme example of a covert

kind of activity. My own sense is we make a
great, great mistake, and we endanger one person
above anyone else, and that's the president, if we
engage in assassination types of techniques, because no foreign government can defeat the
United States Army, but a lot of foreign individuals can come up with ways of killing an individual
American citizen.

In 1968, American soldiers were fighting and dying in the jun-
gles of Southeast Asia. But the Vietnam war didn't start this way.
It started secretly, off the books, like so many of these ventures
that have ended disastrously.

The CIA got there early, soon after the Vietnamese won their
independence from the French in 1954. Eisenhower warned that
the nations of Southeast Asia would fall like dominoes if the
communists, led by Ho Chi Minh, took over all Vietnam. To hold
the line, we installed a puppet regime in Saigon under Ngo Dinh
Diem. American-trained commandoes were used to sabotage
bus and rail lines and contaminate North Vietnam's oil supplies.
The situation kept getting worse.

President Kennedy sent the Green Berets to Vietnam and
turned to full-scale counterinsurgency. As a senator, he had once
said Vietnam was "the ultimate test of our will to stem the tide
of world communism." As president, he sent 15,000 Americans
to be "advisers" there. The secret war was leading to deeper in-
volvement and more deception.

PRES. LYNDON B. JOHNSON (August 4, 1964):
It is my duty to the American people to report
that renewed hostile actions against United States
ships on the high seas in the Gulf of Tonkin have

today required me to order the military forces of
the United States to take action in reply.

This president was not telling the truth, either. The action in
the Gulf of Tonkin was not unprovoked. South Vietnam had been
conducting secret raids in the area against the North, and the
American destroyer ordered into the battle zone had advance
warning it could be attacked. But Johnson seized the incident
to stampede Congress into passing the Gulf of Tonkin Resolution, which he then used as a blank check for the massive
buildup of American forces.

> PROFESSOR FIRMAGE: You have always had presi-
> dents who, as an aberration, will act on their own
> and then afterward look to Congress for authoriza-
> tion retrospectively of their act. But in this case,
> you had a full-dress defense of inherent presiden-
> tial power, inherent executive power, and the
> power as commander in chief to use the Army
> and the Navy whatever way they wanted.

The Constitution is clear on this, too: "Congress shall have the
power to declare war."

April 1965. Two battalions of Marines landed in South Vietnam, the first of more than 2.5 million Americans to fight there
without a congressional declaration of war. The dirty little war
that began in secret was reaching full roar.

> MR. MCGEHEE: We were murdering these people,
> incinerating them.

Ralph McGehee went there for the CIA.

MR. MCGEHEE: My efforts had resulted in the
deaths of many people, and I just — for me it was
a period when I guess I was — I consider myself
nearly insane. I just couldn't reconcile what I had
been and what I was at the time becoming. And
it was so painful for me. It's just hard for me to
express it because I became completely antisocial;
I couldn't deal with anybody. I just was dealing
mentally; it was an internal battle. Every night I
would lie on my bed and think, well, this can't be
true, why are we doing it, why don't we stop, why
don't — why can't we accept — And it was just a
battle all night long, all day long, every minute of
the day I fought this battle over and over again,
and it — and it — to me, suicide became a
longed-for way out of this turmoil that I could see
no other exit from. And finally when I got over
that, I wanted to jump off the agency's hotel, the
Duke Hotel out there, and kill myself, and hang a
banner, "F__ the CIA," or "The CIA lies" or something like that, just to try to bring home, have my
death serve some purpose, to make the American
people realize the truth: they were being lied to.

Many of the secret warriors in Southeast Asia had no such doubts
or regrets. Some of the team that later joined the Iran-contra
enterprise helped run the secret war in Laos. As General Secord
later put it, "Laos belonged to the CIA."

American planes blasted the communists in the jungle, and
on the ground we had our own secret army, the Hmong tribes-
men. The Hmong fought the communists for 15 years while
our secret government made grandiose promises to them about
the future. But we abandoned them to the communist Pathet

Lao in 1975. One-third of the mountain people died. Religious groups helped survivors to escape and brought some of them to Wausau, Wis.

> XIONG LOR: I wouldn't be here if my father and my brothers weren't involved, you know, during the secret war. I am here because I have no choice of being here, and I'd be, like I say, an example here right now, 27 years after, of CIA goof-up. Because they weren't willing to carry through their goals. They think that it was so simple, that people are just like the pawn of a game, like a chess game, you know — that you can move them around anywhere you want, but you have to understand that playing with human life is very different from playing a game because a game, once you lose, there's nothing at stake. But when you lose a person's life, or devastate a whole country, as they did to my country, then it's very important.

During the hearings this summer, Oliver North repeated something we've heard often in the last 40 years, from presidents and the presidents' men.

> COLONEL NORTH: I want you to know lying does not come easy to me. I want you to know that it doesn't come easy to anybody. But I think we all had to weigh in the balance the difference between lives and lies.

But the memories of the mountain people — and the scenes of Saigon's fall — suggest a different equation: the lives lost because we lied to ourselves and to others. Someone always pays for decisions made secretly in Washington. Such pictures bring to mind the words of an old ally, a Vietnamese official who survived the fall of Saigon and escaped to America: "Life and death issues for us were merely bargaining chips in the American pursuit of global policy."

I played a minor role in the Kennedy administration and a much larger one for half the Johnson years. I saw the Peace Corps go forth one day and the Green Berets the next. Once I wrote a speech for LBJ that implied a striking coincidence between the president's wish and God's will. A wise older man from my past called to gently upbraid me. He reminded me that it's very important how we talk about God, because there can be disastrous consequences to what we say. Just so, we've learned that presidents must be very careful talking about what they want this nation to do, because the United States can unhinge whole countries simply by shifting its weight. The passion of the time was that America's defense and security were at stake in Vietnam. But our obsession was the real threat. Vietnam pushed the cold war morality to its extreme conclusion: exorbitant means to accomplish limited ends. Anything goes. The wounds still go deep.

CURTIS L WATSON Jr ·
ROBERT E SMITH Jr ·
EDWARD C WOOD ·
SKYLER L HASUIKE ·
ARTIS W ANDERSON ·
WILLMATT BROWN ·
TERRY W CARPENTER ·
NICOLAS FLORES ·
JOHNNY HARRISON ·
MICHAEL B MAULDIN ·
HAROLD B NADEAU ·
KENNETH W PICKETT ·
BILLY E SNIPES ·
JOHN W TEAGUE ·
WILLIAM WALTERS ·
JOSE YBANEZ ·
JERRY W BELL
FELIDELPHIO B GOMEZ ·
MICHAEL G MERRIMAN ·
RANDOLPH C SCOTT ·
ASTER WATTS ·
EMMET L JOHNSON ·
LEON R SCRIBER ·
CLINTON R BROWN ·
DANIEL KNARIAN ·
GEORGE H STAHL Jr ·
HENRY BENTON ·
JAMES J BROPHY ·
JAMES F BROOKS Jr ·
JOHN R GODERRE ·
MARSHAL J O'NEAL ·
ANTONIO P MACIMINIO ·
CHESTER SCHAPANICK ·
ROBERT H CRUM Jr ·
LAWRENCE E FOSTER ·
JOHN L KOCHENSPARGER ·
ALLEN J RITTER ·
JOSEPH WILSON ·
LOUIS RIDINGS ·
JOHN M BATISTE ·
RONALD L GUYER ·
BOBBY JOE BAREFIELD ·
TERRENCE H GRIFFEY ·
THOMAS J WINKELVOSS ·
JOSEPH L RAPP ·
ALDON M ASHERMAN Jr ·
JAMES W BRILES ·
CLEMENT S CASTALDO ·
DARRELL G DORMAN ·
MICHAEL WATERS
MARCELINO SANTOS-ATEGA
LOUIS X CABRERA Jr
WILLIAM JONES Jr
EDWIN R TRAVNICEK
ROY C McEWEN
REINER W BIEROWSKI
LELAND R COTTIN · FLOYD C DENSON
WAYNE L EVITT · GABRIEL GALLEGOS
ROBERT C JOHNSON · RONNIE LEE JONES
JAMES R McWEE · GARY E OOTHOUDT
GARY L SANGSTER · DONALD F SCHMIDT
EDWIN H SORNSON · JOHN W TUNNELL
MILLARD L WILLIAMSON · JAMES G CONDON III
BRUCE M JOHNSON · BENJAMIN F LIDDELL II
MANUEL A PEREZ-RIVERA · MICHAEL J SOTH
ROBERT C BOICOURT · EDMUND D BRENT Jr
ERVELL M GUEVARA · THOMAS N HARRISON
WILLIAM M KELLY · WILLIAM LUTZ · LARRY LEE PAGE
GARY H ROGERS · SYLVESTER A SCHAEFER
THOMAS E SULLIVAN · PRISHARDO T TORRES · NATHANIEL WILSON
FRANCISCO LUNA · JOHN W CABRERA · FREDDY LEE SAPP
WILLIAM DOWDY · ANTHONY GILMORE · DELL G HAMPTON · JOHN E HAMPTON
JERRY J JOHNSON · JAMES T LESTER · BENTFORD BENNETT
ERNEST E McALUM · GEORGE L McWILLIAMS
RUDOLPH WHITAKER · CHARLES C WILLIAMS · LARRY D WILLIAMS
LLOYD H BRAYE · WILLIE L COLLIER
ALLAN A GANZY · BILLY M GREEN · JOHNNY HICKEY
BOBBY JOE JAMES · RONNIE C JONES
RICHARD F LABARBERA · CARL J LATOUR
MELVIN McCRAY · JURIS PUDULS · ROBERT W REID
WILLIAM R SAVAGE · GORDON R SKYLES
HOLLIS A WALKER · JERRY H WILLIAMS
MILLER J BOURG · EDWARD G CREED
CHARLES M EDWARDS · THOMAS C EDWARDS
ISAAC JONES · LAWRENCE D KESLER
RONALD G McBETH · WILLIAM R REESE Jr
RICHARD L STRANGE · ERNEST W STREHLE
FRANKLIN ALSTON Jr · JAMES COLEMAN Jr
IVOR E BUNCH · JAMES COLEMAN Jr
HACHIRO IMAI · LEWIS J JACKSON
HARRY T RICHARDSON Jr · JACKIE LEE GOFORTH
DONALD R BRYANT · EDWARD K PARSA
BILLY JOE NAVE · DONALD H STAHL
GENE A SMITH · MICHAEL F BINGHAM

3.

"Send in the CIA"

"Send In the CIA"

3.

There are 58,000 names on the wall of the Vietnam memorial; 58,000 men died in Vietnam. Their deaths and all the deaths in Southeast Asia — the names not on this wall — raise painful questions about our secret government and our role in the world. Were we certain what we asked people to die for?

The men who wrote our Constitution tried to make it hard to go to war. Human life was at stake, they knew, as well as the character of this republic. War should be soberly decided, publicly debated, and mutually determined by the people's representatives. It is the people, after all, who must fight, pay, and die once the choice is made. The Constitution was to protect them from dying for the wrong reasons. It was to protect them from killing for the wrong reasons.

> FIRST VIETNAM VETERAN: I don't know, the public still don't want to understand what the hell really happened. But maybe one day they will. As far as Central America, I see the same damn thing happening there in Central America that happened in Vietnam.

SECOND VIETNAM VETERAN: Well, I think the
country has learned very graphically that we better be really assured that if we're going to send
our young men and women off to die like this,
that it better really be in the interests of every
citizen of this United States to sacrifice somebody
like that, so that we don't have more blood on
this wall or other walls. And I think that we ask a
lot of questions now that we didn't used to ask.
We want to know why, and we'll hear Ollie
North's analysis of what's happening with the contras, and a lot of us say we want some more
verification of that. We want to know just what
are we involving ourselves in when we go do that.

I find it stunning, looking back, how easily the cold war enticed
us into surrendering popular control of government to the national security state. We've never come closer to bestowing absolute authority on the president. Setting up White House oper-
atives who secretly decide to fight dirty little wars is a direct
assumption of war powers expressly forbidden by the
Constitution.

Not since December 1941 has Congress declared war. Yet we've
had a "police action" in Korea, "advisers" in Vietnam, "covert
operations" in Central America, "peacekeeping" in Lebanon,
and "low-intensity conflicts" going on right now from Angola
to Cambodia. We're never really sure who is exercising the war
powers of the United States, what they're doing, what it costs,
or who is paying for it. The one thing we are sure of is that
this largely secret global war, carried on with less and less accountability to democratic institutions, has become a way of life.
And now we're faced with a question brand-new in our history:
can we have a permanent warfare state and democracy, too?

In 1975, as the war in Vietnam came to an end, Congress took its first public look at the secret government. Sen. Frank Church chaired the Select Committee to Study Government Operations. The hearings opened the books on a string of lethal activities, from the use of electric pistols and poison pellets to Mafia connections and drug experiments. They gave us a detailed account of assassination plots against foreign leaders and of the overthrow of sovereign governments. We learned, for example, how the Nixon administration had waged a covert war against the government of Chile's president, Salvador Allende, who was ultimately overthrown by a military coup and assassinated.

> SENATOR CHURCH (1976): Like Caesar peering into the colonies from distant Rome, Nixon said the choice of government by the Chileans was unacceptable to the president of the United States. The attitude in the White House seemed to be, "If in the wake of Vietnam I can no longer send in the Marines, then I will send in the CIA."

But the secret government had also waged war on the American people. The hearings examined a long train of covert actions at home, from the bugging of Martin Luther King by the FBI under Kennedy and Johnson to gross violations of the law and of civil liberties in the 1970s. They went under code names such as Chaos, Cable Splicer, Garden Plot, and Leprechaun. According to the hearings, the secret government had been given a license to reach, as journalist Theodore White wrote, all the way to every mailbox, every college campus, every telephone, and every home.

> MORTON HALPERIN: You start out breaking foreign laws since most countries have laws against

secretly overthrowing their governments, and then
you end up breaking the law at home, and com-
ing to feel a contempt for the law, for your col-
leagues and associates, for the Congress and the
public, and for the Constitution.

Morton Halperin was a victim of the secret government's
paranoia. He worked for Henry Kissinger on the National Security Council in 1969. Critical of policies in Cambodia and Vietnam, he resigned. He later discovered his telephone had been
bugged for 21 months. He is now the director of the Washington office of the American Civil Liberties Union.

MR. HALPERIN: What you have is a growing gap
between the perceptions inside the executive
branch about what the threats are to our national
security and the beliefs in the Congress and the
public about the threats to national security. And
that leads to secrecy. That is what drives the
policy underground, that's what leads the president to rely more on covert operations, what
leads the president and his officials to lie to the
public, then lie to the Congress about the operation. Precisely because they cannot get their way
in public debate, they are driven to seek to cir-
cumvent the democratic process.

Oliver North obviously disagrees:

COLONEL NORTH (Iran-contra hearings):
And the president ought not to be in a position,
in my humble opinion, of having to go out and
explain to the American people on a biweekly ba-

sis or any other kind, that I, the president, am
carrying out the following secret operations. It
just can't be done.

In my interview with Professor Firmage, I cited a common
rationale:

MOYERS: It is said that the constitutional system
of checks and balances has so prohibited the
president, so hamstrung him, that he cannot ef-
fectively lead foreign policy, that he has to be
resorting to clandestine, covert, secret —

PROFESSOR FIRMAGE: Horsefeathers. He needs to
do that only when he wants to subvert Congress.
If Congress says, "Don't do that," and the president says, "But I want to, I want to, I really want
to," the conclusion from that isn't that the president is right. It is that the president is consider-
ing being an outlaw.

It's been said that the secret realm of government is the
deformed offspring of the modern presidency. Presidents take
an oath to uphold the Constitution, but then, finding the cum-
bersome sharing of power with Congress an obstacle, they start
looking for shortcuts to silence their critics and achieve their
objectives.

MR. HALPERIN: And it goes back to the beginning.
I mean, there is a famous letter, which Madison
wrote late in his life, in which he said, "Perhaps it
is a universal truth that the loss of liberty at
home will be charged to dangers, real or imag-

ined, from abroad." And that is the lesson of
history.

But we don't seem to learn the lessons of history. Just 15 years
ago, another Senate committee listened to another string of wit-
nesses. The names still trip off the tongue: Haldeman, Ehrlichman, Mitchell, and Dean.

> JOHN DEAN, counsel to the president (Watergate
> hearings, 1973): I began by telling the president
> that there was a cancer growing on the presidency,
> and if the cancer was not removed, the president
> himself would be killed by it.

The White House crimes known as Watergate were crimes
against democracy. To harass opponents, the Nixon White House
had set up a secret team called "the plumbers." They bugged
phones, opened mail, and burglarized the president's critics.
Senator Inouye read the Watergate committee a secret White
House memo containing the Nixon "enemies list" and detail-
ing how the plumbers intended to "use the available federal
machinery to screw our political enemies."
   In both the Watergate and Iran-contra hearings, there was contempt for Congress.

> SEN. SAM J. ERVIN, D-N.C. (Watergate hearings, 1973):
> I believe Congress set up the FBI to determine
> what was going on in this country, didn't it?

> JOHN EHRLICHMAN, assistant to the president:
> Among other things, Mr. Chairman.

> SENATOR ERVIN: It set up the CIA to determine
> what was going on in respect to foreign intelli-
> gence, didn't it?

MR. EHRLICHMAN: Yes, sir, and a number of others.

SENATOR ERVIN: But it didn't set up the plumbers, did it?

MR. EHRLICHMAN: Of course the Congress doesn't do everything, Mr. Chairman.

SENATOR ERVIN: No, but Congress is the only one that's got legislative power, and I don't know anything, any law that gave the president the power to set himself up what some people have called the secret police, namely, the plumbers.

MR. NIELDS (Iran-contra hearings, 1987): What was the reason to withhold information from Congress when they inquired about it?

ADMIRAL POINDEXTER: I simply didn't want any outside interference.

MR. NIELDS: Now, the outside interference you're talking about was Congress, and I take it the reason they were inquiring was precisely so that they could fulfill with information their constitutional function, to pass legislation one way or the other, isn't that true?

ADMIRAL POINDEXTER: Yes, I suppose that's true.

MR. NIELDS: And that you regarded as outside interference.

There was contempt for the law.

> SEN. HERMAN E. TALMADGE, D-Ga. (Watergate hearings, 1973): If the president could authorize a covert break-in, and you don't know exactly where that power would be limited — you don't think it could include murder or other crimes beyond covert break-ins, do you?

> MR. EHRLICHMAN: Oh, I don't — I don't know where the line is, Senator.

> SEN. GEORGE J. MITCHELL, D-Me. (Iran-contra hearings, 1987): During your discussions with Mr. Casey, Mr. McFarlane, and Mr. Poindexter about the plan, did a question ever arise among you as to whether what was being proposed was legal?

> COLONEL NORTH: Oh, no, I don't think it was — I mean, first of all, we operated from the premise that everything we did do was legal.

And there was contempt for the truth.

> SAM DASH, Senate chief counsel (Watergate hearings, 1973): Mr. Mitchell, do you draw a distinction between not volunteering and lying?

> JOHN MITCHELL, former U.S. attorney general: Well, it depends entirely on the subject matter, Mr — .

> MR. DASH: Well, you're asked a direct question, and you don't volunteer a direct answer, you

might say you're not volunteering but actually you are lying on those respects, aren't you?

MR. MITCHELL: Well, I think we'd have to find out what the specifics are of what particular occasion and what case.

SEN. DAVID BOREN, D-Okla. (Iran-contra hearings, 1987): Could you explain to me the difference that you think there is between knowing that you've left a false impression or a wrong impression and lying, to use an old-fashioned term?

ELLIOTT ABRAMS, assistant secretary of state: Yeah, I think lying, we really mean — I mean a deliberate effort to mislead people, a deliberate effort to leave them with a misleading impression. What I hoped to do was to avoid the question and duck the question, as I explained.

And just as there are those today who discount the Iran-contra affair as "politics as usual," there were those who maintained that Watergate was only "more of the same," "something everybody did."

BOSSES OF THE SENATE

Joseph Keppler, 1889

ALTERED DOCUMENT

4.

Corruption
in
Washington:
Then & Now

Corruption in Washington: Then and Now 4.

To put both Watergate and the Iran-contra scandal in perspective, a good place to begin is at 1701 Pennsylvania Avenue, headquarters in 1972 for the Committee to Re-elect the President, or CREEP as it was known. From 1701 Pennsylvania Avenue it's only 345 steps to the White House. Next to the White House is the Executive Office Building, which once housed the Department of War. Within these few blocks, willful and powerful men have plotted some of the worst scandals in our national history. It's worth looking back at them briefly, especially in light of the contention that Watergate and the Iran-contra affair are merely two more strands in the same web of skulduggery. In truth, they are unlike any scandals of the past.

This is not to say that Washington was ever the city described in my civics books. From the beginning, along with the courage and high-mindedness have gone the darndest greed and chicanery the mind can imagine. High ideals compete all the time here with the grubby demons of human nature, usually in the same personality — and they often lose. Monuments turn out to be only marble, presidents only men, and their boy wonders come and go like cherry blossoms in the spring.

So much corruption flourished during the Civil War that an exasperated General Sherman raged at the universal cheating in clothes, blankets, flour, and bread. And Carl Sandburg closed one chapter of his biography of Lincoln with this lament: "The unremitting quest of individual profits and personal fortunes behind warfronts when men were dying for proclaimed sacred causes make a contrast heavy for the human mind to hold and endure."

A century ago, congressmen and bureaucrats would gather at the Willard Hotel two blocks from the White House to hoist their glasses to the hospitality of jobbers looking for government contracts. A predacious character named Jim Fisk summed it up: "You can sell anything to the government at almost any price you've got the guts to ask."

I once asked a historian why Ulysses S. Grant looked so dour in the pictures we see in textbooks. He replied, "You would look dour too if you had his friends." By the time Grant left office, his vice president, the Navy Department, the Department of the Interior, the Diplomatic Service — almost the whole government — were soaked in scandal. Henry Adams would write that for the next 25 years one could search the whole of Congress, the judiciary, and the executive, and find little but damaged reputations. Great fortunes were made through the collaboration of distinguished senators and industrial barons who literally plundered the nation's resources. "You steal a pair of shoes, and you go to jail," Mother Jones said. "You steal a railroad, and you go to the U.S. Senate."

Theodore Roosevelt lowered his lance and charged these citadels of privilege — with some success. "If we've done anything wrong," J.P. Morgan said to the president, "send your man to see my man, and they will fix it up." Roosevelt wanted to stop it, not fix it. In time, Harold Geneen, whose ITT empire might well have turned old J.P. Morgan green with envy, would have better luck; he would send his men to meet with President Nixon's men, and the Justice Department would suddenly drop antitrust proceedings against ITT.

Three blocks north of the White House is 1625 K Street. It's now an office building, but in the 1920s there stood on this site a modest Victorian house known as the headquarters of the Ohio Gang. Friends of Pres. Warren Harding who wanted a favor from the White House, and were willing to pay for it, came here; they could get liquor by the bottle or by the case, even during Prohibition. And thousands of dollars were won and lost in all-night poker games attended by the president himself.

High officials of the Harding administration were frequent visitors to this little green house. In return for a share of the spoils, they hatched a scheme to help a few private oilmen get control of government oil reserves. Their names are not very familiar today, but what they did will long be remembered as the Teapot Dome Scandal.*

Remember the Five Percenters? Officials of the Truman administration, including a high-ranking White House assistant, got government jobs, contracts, and other favors for their friends in return for a commission. And Sherman Adams, President Eisenhower's right-hand man, resigned after it became known he was receiving gifts from a Boston textile merchant in trouble with the regulatory agencies. Not a great deal of money was involved, but in those days people could still get indignant that a public official would accept gratuities from a man who had business with the government.

By the 1970s the ante had gone up, and the motives were different. Two former cabinet officers, John Mitchell and Maurice Stans, were indicted not for receiving money personally

---

* So called because of the physical appearance of one of the oil properties in Wyoming.

but for their role in a $200,000 campaign contribution from a wheeler-dealer wanting help from the Securities and Exchange Commission. Dairy producers kicked in over $300,000 to Nixon's campaign, after which the administration increased price supports, costing consumers $500 million to $700 million in higher milk prices. The president's personal attorney solicited an illegal contribution from American Airlines while the government weighed a decision vitally important to the company; American made the unlawful donation, apparently, because it was afraid not to. Other corporations went along too, buying protection, as it were, from the government.

If this were all there was to it, we could write Watergate off to Original Sin and go on about our business, reminded again of the pernicious side of human nature. But what about everything else Watergate has come to represent: the burglaries and the forgeries, the wiretapping and perjury, the destruction of evidence or the efforts to use the FBI, the CIA, the IRS, and the Secret Service for political purposes? What about the enemies list, the dirty tricks or schemes to obstruct justice, and what about the White House spirit that invested these acts with legitimacy? Such ambitious efforts to discredit the press, to stifle debate in the Executive Branch, to deny the legitimacy of the opposition party, and to humiliate Congress — these were produced by something more, something bigger, than a weakness for the quick buck.

> WILLIAM WHITE, syndicated columnist: Here, you have no strictly monetary motive. You have some gross violations of — of spirit, so to speak. Some people think the theft of however many millions were involved in Teapot Dome was worse — I would think *this* is worse. The money-dishonest politician is less appalling to me than the

integrity-dishonest politician. A great deal of what
occurred here was not indictable. It went to
ethics, it went to morality, it went to decency.
These could be — it's a somewhat pompous term,
but these could be termed "spiritual offenses" —
that is to say, offenses against the spirit of the
country, against the spirit of the way we think the
country ought to go, ought to be. We both know
that politics is extremely rough, but most people
in it do, at some point, recognize a line, admittedly
indefinable, but a line beyond which you just
don't go.

Richard L. Strout, of the Christian Science Monitor, is the only
reporter to have covered the Senate hearings on Teapot Dome
and, 50 years later in the same room, Watergate. For his views
on how Watergate is different, I sought him out in the Senate
Caucus room.

MR. STROUT: Teapot Dome — it started off very
quietly. Secretary Fall came in here. He had long
mustaches; he looked like a barker at a circus. He
was an arrogant man, a landowner. He came here
and denied everything, and he said he'd done a
benefit to the nation in saving this oil. Let's see,
that was in October. Then in February the story
came out, and Fall came in again. He was a
crushed man; he'd taken to drink. He came
through that door and walked up here, leaning on
the stick he had. He'd been exposed. That was the
whole story of it, those two entrances of Fall into
this room.

MOYERS: How was his crime different from the crimes of Watergate?

MR. STROUT: His crime, as crime generally was in those days, was for money and for all the carnal sins, sins of the flesh. He got a very famous little black satchel that had a hundred thousand dollars in it. Now, in Watergate, they're not after money; apparently it's hard to find anybody who's put — got very much money out of this; they're after something else this time. Power. Power. If Watergate had succeeded, you ask yourself what would have happened to our form of government. John Mitchell, the attorney-general — must have read the Constitution, but did he know, does he realize, what the separation of power is? He claimed the inherent right of the president to tap wires of his subordinates, to tap wires without the permission of a court — I would have thought almost anybody would have known that that was unconstitutional. And I use this as an example of the kind of thing that was going on here. Watergate to me represents the culmination of the encroachment on the balance of power, put through by a series of strong-willed subordinates who had their own sense of morality. It was not a money morality; it was a desire to do things, to get power for their team, and they considered this to be moral.

5.

Rise of
the
Imperial
Presidency

Rise of the Imperial Presidency 5.

Growth of the executive power made Watergate possible but by no means inevitable. At the Philadelphia Convention, the Founding Fathers knew they would have to give future presidents latitude to deal with events that couldn't be foreseen in 1787; they fretted over leaving so much to chance, but the failure of the Articles of Confederation convinced them the new Republic needed a strong executive. They would try to check his powers through the watchdogs of Congress and the courts. But there was no good alternative, they decided, to a president with a largely unwritten mandate.

Does the presidency today bear any resemblance to what Washington and the other Founding Fathers conceived it to be? I put this question to James David Barber of Duke University, an authority on the office of the presidency.

PROFESSOR BARBER: I know it's much bigger and much more powerful, and so forth and so on, but it's still the number-one office; it's still the focus of feeling, the focus of patriotism, the focus of a lot of political emotion. Washington had a tremendous influence on the respect that Americans still have about the presidency. When the Constitutional Convention was meeting and trying to decide whether to have a monarchy or whether to have the president elected by Congress, as they voted to do five times during the convention, there sat George Washington, who all of them knew would be the first president. Being pragmatic people, as they were, they were much influenced by the presence of that man. They knew he was going to start it off. They were willing to write the provisions in the Constitution for the presidency in very general language. I think that's been important because it's left a lot of leeway for presidents, from Washington to Nixon, to fill in the blanks in the Constitution with their own ways, their own purposes, their own personalities.

The cold war in particular gave modern presidents one opportunity after another to assume unilateral powers. Whether hot or cold, a wartime mentality breeds secrecy, enhances the role of the president as commander in chief, and makes objectives simple and absolute: there's no substitute for victory; it's "us" against "them," and the only goal is to win, with no quarter asked or given.

Listen to Henry Steele Commager, distinguished professor of history at Amherst University:

PROFESSOR COMMAGER: The cold war, beginning about '47, induced a kind of paranoia that we were a beleaguered people under constant threat of attack; that we were surrounded by enemies —

something of the paranoia that Germany had
when Hitler came in — enemies in Russia and
enemies, of course, in Japan — in China as well;
and that it was essential — to build up an enormous military, to resort to secrecy, to use the
weapons that the communists used in order to
fight communism. This was a cross between the
Kafka world and the Orwell world, where you
defeat your enemies by using their weapons, and
using their weapons perhaps more lavishly and
more recklessly than they themselves are prepared to use them.

MOYERS: What led to using in domestic politics
those tactics that have been employed abroad?

PROFESSOR COMMAGER: Ah, that was very easy. I
think that began, really, with McCarthy and
McCarthyism* — the notion that America was in-

---

* McCarthy, Joseph R. (1908–57), Republican senator from Wisconsin
(1947–57). In 1950, during a speech on Lincoln's Birthday in Wheeling, W.
Va., he waved a piece of paper at his audience and said, "I have here in my
hand a list of 205 persons that were known to the secretary of state as being
members of the Communist party and who nevertheless are still working
and shaping policy of the State Department." He awoke the next morning
to find himself a national figure, and his extraordinary ability to generate
fear and suspicion was to infect American politics for the next four years.
Seeing communism as an issue that might ensure his re-election, McCarthy
proceeded to exploit fears of a "Red tide," pressing his accusations in 1954
through months-long televised hearings into alleged communist influence
in the Army. A Senate subcommittee found McCarthy's original charges "a
fraud and a hoax," and in December 1954 the Senate voted 67–22 to censure
him for contempt of the Senate. But for more than a year before that time,
McCarthy's reckless attacks virtually paralyzed policymaking in Washington. Subsequently, "McCarthyism" came into the language as shorthand for
any political effort to rule through lies and intimidation, and for the general
hysteria that such an effort can produce.

fected with communism. We kind of became en-
meshed in conspiratorial psychology, where
McCarthy persuaded large segments of the American people that there was a communist under
your bed at night, that the teachers were communists, that the clergy were communists, that
bureaucrats were communists, that, indeed, the
Communist party was almost as large as the
Democratic and Republican, but all-secret, and
therefore had to be rooted out.

For a long time national politics were to be infected with a war-
like passion that warped men's judgment and wounded the spirit
of civility that was supposed to temper our politics. Opponents
were not just other politicians, competing legitimately for an
office. They were somehow linked to international conspiracies,
and politics was war waged as a crusade.

Just as significantly, the cold war concentrated in the White
House almost unlimited discretion to define the national security. Actually, national security turned out to be a concept easier
to act upon than define. In World War II, it hadn't been necessary to spell it out; Hitler and Pearl Harbor had done that for
us. Lyndon Johnson and Richard Nixon both served in that war,
when patriotism was simply defined as support for the commander in chief in a time of clear-cut danger. But they would
come to power in a world befogged with paradox and ambiguity;
as presidents, they would be frustrated and riled as millions of
Americans refused to accept their word that Vietnam was vital
to national security. Such a challenge to the commander in chief
had been simply unthinkable when their views were shaped
in the 1940s, and in the 1960s they would take the challenge
personally.

"I'm the commander in chief," Johnson once said, watching

demonstrators on television. "Why are they doing this to me?"

At first, "they" were Nervous Nellies, but in the end they were thought to be subversive, subject to widespread military surveillance.

By now the events of the sixties had created a fierce and unbridled momentum, and Nixon would reach the White House in a time of raging intemperance. The ruling passion in those years had been for everyone to do his own thing, to gratify his own appetites by any means necessary. For fanatics, this meant a gun in the crowd to settle a personal score against the world. For die-hard segregationists, it meant fire hoses against civil-rights demonstrators and defiance at schoolhouse doors. For political extremists, it meant a bomb in a public building to make the world safe for idealism. And for the government, it became exorbitant means to accomplish limited ends.

The war Nixon inherited untied dark and brutal forces and gave them official legitimacy. "This is not a conventional war," said the colonel who served as foreman on one of the My Lai juries. "We have to forget propriety."

And we did.

At first the aims of the war seemed to a lot of us worthy and intelligible. But an Army major, standing in ruins and ashes, finally summed up what had gone wrong. "It became necessary to destroy this town," he told a reporter, "to save it."

Excess abroad provoked excess at home. Rage met rage until the whole nation seemed to have abandoned the protocol of law.

JEB MAGRUDER, deputy director, Office of Communications (Watergate hearings, 1973): During this whole period of time that we were in the White House,
— we were directly employed for the purpose of trying to succeed with the president's policies, and I knew how he was trying very diligently to

settle the war issue, and we were all at that time
against the war. As an example (I think this is a
primary issue), we saw continual violations of the
law done by men like William Sloane Coffin.*
Now he tells me my ethics are bad, and yet *he*
was indicted for criminal charges; he recom-
mended on the Washington Monument grounds
that students burn their draft cards. I respect Mr.
Coffin tremendously; he was a very close friend
of mine. [But] I saw people that I was very close
to breaking the law without any regard for any
other person's pattern of behavior or belief. And I
believed as firmly as they did that the president
was correct in this issue. So consequently, and let
me just finish, when these subjects came up, and
although I was aware they were illegal, and I'm
sure the others did, we were accomplishing what
we thought was a cause, a legitimate cause.

But civil disobedience, of the sort William Sloane Coffin
preached and practiced, was done in the open by people willing to take the consequences; it was not done secretly, from
behind the shield of executive privilege, by trusted officials sworn
to uphold the law.

Government was supposed to protect society against lawlessness; now it became a lawbreaker, violating the Constitution,
in effect, in order to save it. What one senator called "a lethal
mutation" occurred in the idea of national security. Anyone who
disagreed with the view espoused by Jeb Magruder and his col-
leagues that the president was right became suspect. If the presi-

---

* The Rev. William Sloane Coffin, Jr., then chaplain, Yale University. At Williams College, where in the late fifties he taught a course in ethics, Magruder
was one of his students.

dent's word were the infallible last word on national security and he were the only one to save it, then re-electing the president was essential to the nation's survival. Anyone who questioned his word could be labeled a traitor.

The distinction between the president and the country paled, and critics of official policy became a threat not only to the republic but to his personal psyche.

> JOHN DEAN (Watergate hearings, 1973): I was made aware of the president's strong feeling about even the smallest of demonstrations during the late winter of 1971, when the president happened to look out the window of the residence of the White House and saw a lone man with a large 10-foot sign stretched out in front of Lafayette Park.
>
> Mr. Higby* called me to his office to tell me that the president's — of the president's displeasure with the sign in the park and told me that Mr. Haldeman had said that the sign had to come down.
>
> When I came out of Mr. Higby's office, I ran into Dwight Chapin,** who said he was going to get some thugs to remove the man from Lafayette Park. He said it would take him a few hours to get them, but they could do the job.
>
> I told him I didn't believe that was necessary.

In New York City, on May 8, 1970, angry construction workers attacked a group of antiwar demonstrators. Three weeks later,

---

* Lawrence M. Higby, administrative assistant to Robert Haldeman.
** Dwight L. Chapin, appointments secretary for President Nixon.

leaders of these construction workers were invited to the White House to be personally thanked by President Nixon for their support of his Vietnam policies. If any of the young men on his staff needed a sign that tough measures against the president's opponents were okay, this was it. Extremism in the defense of the White House was no vice. They went after it with gusto. The enemies list grew.

But were they enemies of the president—or enemies of the state? It was hard to discriminate, and Dean proposed that the machinery of government be used to screw them all. White House agents went after Daniel Ellsberg,* and the president's men hired agents to sabotage the Democratic primaries and assure Nixon's election.

I spent four and a half years in the White House and can testify as to how tempting it is to put the president's interests above all others. You begin to confuse the office with the man and the man with the country. Life inside those iron gates takes on an existential quality. "I think with the president's mind; therefore I am."

To some extent this happens in every administration. But the men in and around the Nixon White House were measured by their zeal.

> JOHN CAULFIELD, CREEP employee: I felt very strongly about the president, extremely strongly about the president. I was very loyal to his people that I worked for. I place a high value upon loyalty.

---

* Dr. Daniel J. Ellsberg, an official in the Defense Department in the Johnson administration, in 1970 admitted to having released to the press a copy of the top-secret Pentagon Papers, a massive study of the U.S. role in Indochina commissioned by Defense Secretary Robert McNamara.

BERNARD BARKER, Watergate spy: Sure. I am
not — I wasn't there to think. I was there to follow orders, not to think.

HERBERT PORTER, scheduling director, CREEP: My
loyalty to this man, Richard Nixon, goes back
longer than [that for] any person that you will see
sitting at this table throughout any of these
hearings.

H.R. HALDEMAN, White House chief of staff: Those
who served with me at the White House had
complete dedication to the service of this country.
They had great pride in the president they served
and great pride in the accomplishments of the
Nixon administration in its first four years.

MR. EHRLICHMAN: I do not apologize for my
loyalty to the president any more than I apologize
for my love of this country. I only hope that my
testimony here has somehow served them both.

ATTORNEY GENERAL MITCHELL: And I was not
about to countenance anything that would stand
in the way of that re-election.

This loyalty was given not only to the man but to the cause,
and the cause reflected the old American will to win — with
a modern twist.

   "When the one great scorer comes to write against your name,
he marks not that you won or lost, but how you played the game."
The sportswriter Grantland Rice formulated that ethic in 1923.
In theory, at least, the name of the game was fair play.

By the 1960s, football had a new ethic, articulated by Vince Lombardi of the Green Bay Packers and Washington Redskins.

"Winning isn't everything," Lombardi said. "It's the only thing."

In the situation room of CREEP, a windowless, well-guarded command post across from the committee's headquarters, the president's team hung a sign borrowed from the president's favorite coach: "Winning in politics isn't everything; it's the only thing."

The name of the game was victory.

> SENATOR TALMADGE (Watergate hearings, 1973): Am I to understand from your response that you placed the expediency of the next election above your responsibility as an intimate adviser to the president of the peril that surrounded him? Did you state that the expediency of the election was more important than that?

> ATTORNEY GENERAL MITCHELL: In my mind, the re-election of Richard Nixon, compared with what was available on the other side, was so much more important that I put it in just that context.

Whatever they thought about the public mood, the men linked to Watergate clearly thought they were doing what the president wanted. They cloaked their criminal deeds in a boundless notion of national security, and by the president's own admission they got that notion from him.

This is the president's statement of May 22, 1973: "Because of the emphasis I put on the crucial importance of protecting the national security, I can understand how highly motivated individuals could have felt justified in engaging in specific activities that I would have disapproved had they been brought to my attention."

Yet two years earlier, in 1970, the president personally had approved the use of clandestine techniques he had been warned were illegal: a secret intelligence operation coordinated by a White House assistant who was authorized to use surreptitious entry and other unlawful methods, in clear violation of the Constitution. The staff memorandum approved by the president spelled it out:

> SENATOR ERVIN (Watergate hearings, 1973): "Use of this technique," the document states, "is clearly illegal. It amounts to burglary. It is also highly risky. And could result in great embarrassment if exposed. However, it is also the most fruitful tool and can produce the type of intelligence which cannot be obtained in any other fashion." Now, that's what the record shows.

The president later established a secret police operation in the White House basement. Its agents would bypass the regular investigating agencies of the government to engage in criminal acts.

Breaking the law was not out of bounds. What the Constitution forbade, the president could permit.

> SENATOR TALMADGE (Watergate hearings, 1973): If the president could authorize a covert break-in, you don't know exactly where that power would be limited. You don't think it could include murder or other crimes beyond covert break-ins, do you?

MR. EHRLICHMAN: I don't know where the line is, Senator.

There, in brief, is the Watergate morality embedded in the Nixon White House: belief in the total rightness of the official view of reality and an arrogant disregard for the rule of law — the triumph of executive decree over due process.

Given what we have learned of the secret sale of arms to Iran and of the private war in Nicaragua, were these on a par with Watergate? Once again, hear Professor Firmage:

PROFESSOR FIRMAGE: Oh, the substance of it is far above Watergate. You have the sale of armaments to terrorist groups, which can only foment more kidnapping and more terror, and finance it. You have the doing of this by members of the armed forces, a very scary thing. You have the government, in part at least, put in motion doing things that Congress has forbidden — direct illegality. You have constitutional abuses that are enormous.

6.

The
Shredding
of
Democracy

The
Shredding
of Democracy 6.

PRES. RICHARD NIXON (East Room, the White
House, August 8, 1974): I shall resign the presidency,
effective at noon tomorrow.

Watergate drove Richard Nixon from office. The Imperial
Presidency was down but not out.

Ronald Reagan ran in 1980 with a strong and clear message:
the world was a hostile place and closing in on America. Rus-
sian troops were in Afghanistan, Sandinistas were in Nicaragua,
and Americans were being held hostage in Iran. President
Reagan wanted to reinvigorate the CIA. To run it, he chose a
tough director, his campaign manager, William Casey.

They were ideological soulmates, true Cold Warriors on the
offensive. In seven years Reagan approved over 50 major covert
operations, more than any president since John F. Kennedy.
Reagan and Casey set the agenda, but it was Oliver North's job
to carry it out. In North, they had their 007.

North's primary mission was to keep the contra war going
despite the congressional ban on aid. For two years he master-

minded a privately funded airlift to Honduras. According to some reports, criminal elements seized opportunities presented by the secret airlift to smuggle drugs back into the United States, with profits being used to buy more weapons for the contras.

> SENATOR JOHN KERRY: Were there contras who relied on the profits of narcotics in order to buy arms and to survive? Yes. I'm convinced of that. Once you open up a clandestine network which has the ability to deliver weapons or other goods from this country, leaving airfields secretly under the sanction of a "covert operation," with public officials, DEA, Customs, law enforcement, whatever, pulled back because of the covert sanctioning, you've opened the pipeline for nefarious types who are often involved in these kinds of activities to become the people who bring things back in.

North had been told the airlift was using questionable characters. Robert Owen, his contact man with the contras, wrote from the field that some of the leaders were running drugs. In February 1986, Owen advised North that a resupply plane had been used for shipping drugs. In Owen's words, "Part of the crew had criminal records."

> SEN. DANIEL K. INOUYE, D.-Hawaii (Iran-contra hearings, 1987): The second sentence says, "Nice group the boys choose." Who are the boys?

> MR. OWEN: CIA.

So what happens? I asked Senator Kerry: "In effect, does the president of the United States say, 'This is the national security,

you must step back and let these people do their job,' and therefore a lot of smugglers, drug traffickers, others, go through the
back door?"

> SENATOR KERRY: I don't think the president of the
> United States said specifically, "Look the other
> way to these things." I don't think the president of
> the United States knew these things were going
> on. But the president of the United States did en-
> courage to such a degree the continuation of aid
> to the contras, and it was so clear, through Casey
> and Poindexter, etc., that this was going to please
> the president if it happened. It's clear that there
> were those who turned their heads and looked
> the other way because they knew that this major
> goal was out there and it was part of it, and if
> there happened to be these minor aberrations, as
> people referred to them, that was the price you
> were paying in the effort to accomplish the larger
> goal. Which larger goal, obviously, was against the
> law and against the wishes of the Congress and
> against the American people.

How does it happen that to be anticommunist we become un-
democratic, as if we have to subvert our society in order to save
it? Because the powers claimed by presidents in national security have become the controlling wheel of government, driv-
ing everything else. Secrecy then makes it possible for the president to pose as the sole competent judge of what will best protect our security. Secrecy permits the White House to control
what others know. How many times have we heard a president
say, "If you only knew what I know, you would understand why
I'm doing what I'm doing." But it's a self-defeating situation. As

Lord Acton said, "Everything secret degenerates, even the administration of justice." So in the bunker of the White House, the men who serve the president put loyalty above analysis. Judgment yields to obedience. Just salute and follow orders.

> COLONEL NORTH (Iran-contra hearings, 1987): This lieutenant colonel is not going to challenge a decision of the commander in chief, for whom I still work, and I am proud to work for that commander in chief. And if the commander in chief tells this lieutenant colonel to go stand in the corner and sit on his head, I will do so.

That notion troubled Inouye, a combat hero of World War II. He reminded North of the military code, of a soldier's duty.

> SENATOR INOUYE (Iran-contra hearings, 1987): The uniform code makes it abundantly clear that it must be the lawful orders of a superior officer. In fact it says, "Members of the military have an obligation to disobey unlawful orders." This principle was considered so important that we — we, the government of the United States, proposed that it be internationally applied in the Nuremberg trials. And so in the Nuremberg trials we said that the fact that the defendant —

> BRENDAN SULLIVAN, counsel to Colonel North: Mr. Chairman, may I please register an objection?

> SENATOR INOUYE: May I continue my statement?

MR. SULLIVAN: I find this offensive. I find you're engaging in a personal attack on Colonel North, and you're far removed from the issues of this case.

North's lawyer deflected Inouye, but some of North's fellow officers watching on television took issue with the colonel.

GEORGE GORMAN, former captain, U.S. Marine Corps: I'm two years senior to Oliver North out of the Naval Academy, and the only thing he's got on me is a Silver Star and six more years in the Corps. And when Oliver North started to say the things he started to say, I literally wanted to throw things at my TV set. I seriously considered mailing my Naval Academy ring back to the Naval Academy and denying ever having gone there. I was so embarrassed and humiliated that a professional military officer would stoop to the dishonor and disgrace and warmongering that Oliver North and Poindexter and McFarlane and the rest of the crew did. Selling arms to the Iranians after they blew up the Beirut barracks, after they blew up the Beirut embassy, is the most immoral thing — that's like selling Zyklon-B to the Germans after you've found out the Holocaust is under way.

ROBERT COLCLASURE, former captain, U.S. Marine Corps: One of my drill instructors in the Marine Corps — [it was at a time when] there were a lot of protests in Washington, D.C., and somebody said, well, those commie lovers, or whatever — and the drill instructor told us something as we were about to graduate. He said, "What you're fighting for might be wrong or right, nobody really knows. But," he said, "there's a Constitution that allows those people to be out on the streets protesting." He said, "That's what's worth fighting for. That's what the Constitution is." He said, "That's what you took an oath to, and when you put those bars on as a second lieutenant, you better remember that." I don't think Oliver North had that drill instructor.

It was career military men who managed the Iran-contra debacle under Reagan and Casey; North, Poindexter, McFarlane, Secord, and Singlaub were trained to fight wars, not run foreign policy. In war, the aim is absolute and simple: destroy the enemy, no matter what. They had little understanding of politics in Iran, in Nicaragua, and, most important, in Washington. Yet our foreign policy has increasingly become a military policy. Reagan has doubled the number of military men on the staff of the National Security Council. What was created in 1947 as a civilian advisory group to the president has become a command post for covert operations run by the military. Far removed from public view and congressional oversight, they are accountable only to the one man they serve. The framers of the Constitution feared this permanent state of war, with the commander in chief served by an elite private corps that put the claims of the sovereign above the Constitution.

SENATOR MITCHELL (Iran-contra hearings, 1987):
This is the first page of an order signed and approved by President Reagan.

Mitchell is pointing to the ultimate weapon of the secret government, the National Security Decision Directive, the NSDD. Every president since Harry Truman has issued such directives. Reagan has signed at least 280, covering everything from outer space to nuclear weapons to covert operations in Iran and Nicaragua. In essence, by an arbitrary and secret decree, the president can issue himself a license to do as he will, where he will; and the only ones who need to know are the secret agents who carry it out, the Knights of the Oval Office.

> SENATOR MITCHELL (Iran-contra hearings, 1987): You have testified that, as a member of the National Security Council staff, you conducted a covert operation, and my question is, did the president specifically designate the National Security Council staff for that purpose?

> COLONEL NORTH: I think what I have said consistently is that I believe that the president has the authority to do what he wants with his own staff, that I was a member of his staff, that Mr. McFarlane was, and that Admiral Poindexter was, and in pursuing the president's foreign policy goals of support for the Nicaraguan resistance, he was fully within his rights to send us off to talk to foreign heads of state, to seek the assistance of those foreign heads of state to use other than U.S. government moneys, and to do so without a finding.

"Without a finding." The law requires presidents to make a finding that the national interests will be served by a covert action and to report it to Congress in a timely fashion. The idea is to make sure that both Congress and the executive, each elected independently by the people, are accountable for what is done in our name. But Reagan gave himself permission to ignore the requirements of the law: when he sold arms to our avowed enemy in Iran, he signed the finding after the fact and then ordered that it not be reported to Congress. The president becomes his own arbiter of the law in matters of national security. Or, in Richard Nixon's words, "When the president does it, that means it is not illegal."

> COLONEL NORTH (Iran-contra hearings, 1987): I think it is very important for the American people to understand that this is a dangerous world, that we live at risk, and that this nation is at risk in a dangerous world.

> PROF. STEPHEN F. COHEN, Princeton University: The issue here is not whether we should pursue a foreign policy that guards against the Soviet Union. That's not the issue, because obviously in significant ways the Soviet Union represents a threat to our interests around the world and to our values. The problem is the excessive American perception of that threat, the pathological ways we construe that threat, and what it leads us to do. Because in addition to distorting our domestic priorities, to undermining our democratic civil liberties at home, in the end, arguably, it actually does damage to our national security.

There is, I reminded Professor Firmage, a doctrine called "the reason of state," which holds that whatever is necessary to defend the state's survival must be done by the individuals responsible for it. "Doesn't that," I asked, "take precedence over this 18th-century set of values?"

PROFESSOR FIRMAGE: I think the survival of the state is what the Constitution is about. The reason of state argument is a very slippery thing, and at heart, at best amoral.

MOYERS: Amoral?

PROFESSOR FIRMAGE: Oh, you bet. I would say it ranges from amoral on the good side, to just basically immoral.

MOYERS: Assume I'm president, and I'm going to say, Professor Firmage, that's all wonderful, but I deal in an ugly world. The United States is a wonderful place, relatively, because of this document, because of the values the founders inculcated in us, but the world beyond these borders is a pretty ugly world. People don't like us, people don't share those values, people are out to get us. And if I don't do the ugly things that are necessary to protect us from an ugly world, you won't be able to exercise the right of free speech out at that university." — or horsefeathers'

PROFESSOR FIRMAGE: I would say poppycock, Mr. President. That is simply nonsense. The whole fight is over means, not ends. Every president with every good intention, and every tyrant, with whatever his intention, has used precisely the same argument. That is, don't constrain me by

means, and I will get you there safely and well.
And I think any time we accept a reason of state
argument to justify means that are totally incon-
gruent with the values of our state, we're on the
high road to tyranny and we deserve to be there.

Our nation was born in rebellion against tyranny. We are the
fortunate heirs of those who fought for America's freedom and
then drew up a remarkable charter to protect it against arbitrary
power. The Constitution begins with the words, "We the people." The government gathers its authority from the people, and
the governors are as obligated to uphold the law as the governed.
That was revolutionary. Listen now to the voices of some people who believe the fight for freedom isn't over.

ROGER WILKINS, writer, former U.S. assistant
attorney general: I am a citizen of this country.
That's the highest thing you can be, and you'd
better tell me the truth because we don't run a
secret country, and we don't run a secret
government.

Roger Wilkins and his family have long battled for a more just
America.

MR. WILKINS: And if we continue these policies,
to rob ourselves in order to feed this national
security monster, we are going to continue to degrade American life. That's not real national security. National security for the United States is
making the United States a good place to live,
where people want to be active, intelligent, involved citizens. For people at the top to say, "This

world is so complicated and so dangerous, just a
few of us need to govern it and hold the secrets
in and we will tell you what's good for you," that
is moving down the road to dictatorship.

SCOTT ARMSTRONG: The national security argument now interferes with every American's right
to understand its government. That's what secrecy's all about these days.

Scott Armstrong is director of the National Security Archive, a
public interest group devoted to a more open government. He
has pored over the Iran-contra evidence and believes Congress
has failed to deal with the fundamental constitutional issues.

MR. ARMSTRONG: The Founding Fathers never intended for George Washington to be able to go to
George III and say, "I don't like what Congress
has done here. Give me some money, I'll hire
some mercenaries, and we'll call it American foreign policy." That would have been treason.

Gail Jensen, Marylee Fithian, and Nancy Jones live in Min-
neapolis. Last summer they organized citizens around the state
to monitor the Iran-contra hearings as a way of increasing public awareness.

MARYLEE FITHIAN: The church I go to, we have a
hymn and the words go something like, "I wish
that my eyes had never been opened." Because if
they'd been opened, I'd have to do something
about it, and I think that that's a problem with a
lot of people in this country: they don't want their

eyes to be opened because they're very comfort-
able, very secure; and if their eyes are opened,
they're going to have to do something.

NANCY JONES: The people that we're talking to
have quite — they recognize that we're only talking about subverting the Constitution, that's all.

GAIL JENSEN: The American people are part of
the checks and balances. It's not just the executive branch and the Congress and the judicial
branch; the people have a role too.

PETE EDSTROM: I grew up just feeling. . .the system out here's pretty hunky-dory; all you have to
do is admire it and respect it and let it keep operating. We'll always have freedom, we'll always
have democracy, we'll always have free elections.
[Now] I've got to question. . .[if] that's going to
continue—unless I decide to go for it and keep on
effecting change.

Pete Edstrom, a dairy farmer in Wisconsin, is a believer in the
American way. With his pastor and other farmers, he started
a newspaper to rally their neighbors to community action.

MR. EDSTROM: If there's anything I want my children to understand, it's the concept of the old
town meeting type of politics where people do it,
people are involved, people are informed. I think
that probably the problems this country are in
right now — the [Iran-contra] hearings are a clas-

sic example — are clearly a case of an American people not having been involved.

Walter Chilsen is a Republican state senator in Wisconsin, a popular conservative who says the hearings this summer forced him to reconsider his support for U.S. policy in Central America.

> SEN. WALTER JOHN CHILSEN: When you've been a Republican for 20 years, and you like to say that the Republicans are the best guys, the guys in the white hats, — the recognition that indeed in this very important situation, that *wasn't* the case, that the policy was dead wrong, [makes me feel] an obligation to speak out.

Senator Chilsen's change of heart was personal and political. At the urging of their daughter, Liz, Senator Chilsen and his wife went to Central America to see for themselves. When they returned, he was still critical of the Sandinistas in Nicaragua, but he was also convinced that an American-backed war on peasants was not the way to stop communism.

> SENATOR CHILSEN: There's a great danger that in this country we would accept automatically things that are said to us in a doctrinaire fashion—you know, that we've got to be fighting communism — That can be the whitewash that can cover up a multitude of sins. . . . We can't be fighting for democracy in Central America and — seeing it shredded back here at home.

President Reagan's men did learn one thing from Watergate. Richard Nixon said it only last year: "Just destroy all the tapes."

MR. NIELDS (Iran-contra hearings, 1987): Where are these memoranda?

COLONEL NORTH: Which memoranda?

MR. NIELDS: The memoranda that you sent up to Admiral Poindexter, seeking the president's approval.

COLONEL NORTH: I think I shredded most of that. Did I get them all? I'm not trying to be flippant, I'm just —

MR. NIELDS: Well, that was going to be my very next question, Colonel North. Isn't it true that you shredded them?

COLONEL NORTH: I believe I did.

It doesn't have to be. The people who wrote this Constitution lived in a world more dangerous than ours. They were surrounded by territory controlled by hostile powers, on the edge of a vast wilderness. Yet they understood that even in perilous times, the strength of self-government was public debate and public consensus. They knew too that men are fallible, themselves included, and prone to abuse great office. They left us safeguards against men whose appetites for power might exceed their moral wisdom.

To forget this — to ignore the safeguards, to put aside our basic values out of fear, to imitate the foe in order to defeat him — is to shred the distinction that makes us different. For, in the end, not only our values but our methods separate us from the enemies of freedom. The decisions we make are inherent in the methods that produce them. An open society cannot survive a secret government. Constitutional democracy is no romantic notion. It's our defense against ourselves, the one foe who might defeat us.

Afterword

It is Super Bowl Sunday. A few days earlier someone had asked me, "Honestly, what did all that Iran-contra stuff have to do with the Constitution? And why should I care anyway?" Now, as I watch the game's officials huddling to assess an infraction of the rules, a better answer comes to mind than I gave at the time.

I am struck that during the game not one of the referees consults the rule book. The rules are so interwoven into their experience that any official knows almost instantly which one applies to a given situation. The referees appear to sense intuitively when the intended bounds of the game — the arrangement of the rules — have been offended. They cannot think of the game apart from the rules. Nor can the players. The rules are second nature to them, the intricate warp and woof of the sport. Without them there would be no game. There would simply be hand-to-hand fighting in a pitched battle where the result would be decided by brute strength and cunning. By agreeing to play by the rules, the teams have not decided the outcome of the game, but they have determined the kind of game they will play.

When the Founders of the American republic agreed on the Constitution, they determined the kind of nation this was to be. It was not to be home to arbitrary power. The rules would see to it. The playing field of government was to be level, and the three players — the executive, legislative, and judiciary — would be guided by ethical and constitutional constraints. Each was empowered to blow the whistle on the others if they failed to play by the rules.

Thus the Constitution is essentially a procedural document; the Framers did not prescribe future policies for the country but the manner of choosing what those policies should be. For example, the Constitution does not say the United States cannot go to war. As Edwin Firmage explains in *The War Powers and the Doctrine of Political Questions*, the Framers understood that the reasons for going to war must be left for every generation to work through within the political branches of government. Whether the United States should go to war and under what conditions are political questions. But the way to go to war is not. The Founders put that in the Constitution, our basic book of rules. They gave Congress the power "to declare war and to grant letters of marque and reprisal" (government commissions authorizing privateers to seize enemy vessels).

Their intent was clear. James Madison sat through the entire Constitutional Convention and kept the most thorough record of it. He wrote that the executive branch "is the department of power most distinguished by its propensity to war; hence it is the practice of all states, in proportion as they are free, to disarm this propensity of its influence." To Thomas Jefferson, the Framers had indeed "given one effectual check to the dog of war by transferring the power of letting him loose from the executive to the legislative body, from those who are to spend to those who are to pay." Alexander Hamilton, the chief advocate of presidential power in the Philadelphia convention, nonetheless recognized that since the president lacked the British Crown's authority to declare war and raise armies, his power "would amount to nothing more than the supreme command and direction of the military forces."

Thus the president was given no power to authorize private war, whether declared or undeclared, whether fought with regular public forces or by buccaneers and soldiers of fortune. The declaration of war was to be a public and collegial act — in no small part because in a republic those who will the end must will the means to that end, accepting responsibility for the consequences of their choices.

This emphasis on how the game of statecraft is played is critical to understanding the threat to our constitutional order from the events described in "The Secret Government" and in the House and Senate select committees' report on the Iran-contra scandal, which was released a week after my broadcast. Both assume that in a democracy the means are as important as the ends we seek. Both affirm the notion expressed by public philosopher Reinhold Niebuhr that "the temper and the integrity with which the political fight is waged is more important for the health of our society than any particular policy."

A lawless government is a contradiction in terms. Leaders cannot expect citizens to act lawfully if they themselves act unlawfully. Yet, in sponsoring a private war to overthrow the Nicaraguan regime, the administration consistently subverted our constitutional process. The president did not take care that the laws were faithfully executed. Congress was not permitted to exercise the power of the purse, nor was it notified of executive actions as required by law. Moreover, the president lied to the American people while his subordinates deceived the people's representatives. This gave the White House free rein to manipulate and distort the facts, escaping accountability to the public and undermining "the temper and the integrity" of the political fight.

By its own definition the Reagan administration was to be conservative. But in their contempt for the law, the president and his men stood conservatism on its head. In the words of one former White House assistant, Linda Chavez, "Ollie North is no conservative. There is a world of difference between conservatism and the kind of gung-ho radicalism that allows no obstacle to be put in the path of achieving one's ends. Zealots have no place in democratic governments, for they threaten the very institutions they claim they want to protect."

But the zealots were taken into the heart of government and, in their pursuit of ends by any means, were cheered on by conservative and neoconservative intellectuals and polemicists. Trumpeting adherence to the original intent of the Constitution, for example, they twisted like circus contortionists over the Founders' unequivocal intention that no president was to make war at his pleasure.

Sadly, the triumph of ideology over constitutionality has real-life consequences. The Founders knew about war. It is ultimate in its demands. One's money can be refunded if the government errs in withholding taxes; a solder's limb and life, once lost, are irretrievable, and such sacrifice was not to be asked on whim. Ancient Athens, which some of our Founders considered a worthy model for the new American republic, could not go to war, could not demand that any of its citizens risk their lives for it in war, without securing the agreement of citizens in assembly. As John Dunn writes in his recent *Western Political Theory in the Face of the Future*, "No Athenian citizen could be required to go off to fight for his country and perhaps to die for it, without having at least the formal opportunity to address his fellow citizens on the merits of the venture before he did."

Nor can the issue be solely one of the warrior's sacrifice. Citizens have a moral responsibility for the decisions made by their government that lead to the death of other people. This is why capital punishment can be inflicted only through the application of due process, which owes its legitimacy to democratic governance. Why should our leaders expect us to condone other killing in our name except when a state of war exists or the survival of the nation is at risk?

Yet as I write, the press is reporting another raid by contra guerrillas on yet another farm cooperative in rural Nicaragua. Attacking before dawn, they moved through the center of the village, spraying homes with gunfire. Among the victims were a mother, a father, and two children huddled inside their hut. If this had been the work of the PLO in Israel, or the IRA in Northern Ireland, or the Hezbollah in Beirut, we would condemn it as terrorism. But because the contras are anticommunists — or so we are told by their sponsors — we are to praise *these* killings as freedom fighting.

How ironic it is that having lectured us for years on the plague of moral relativism, these conservatives are now the chief carriers of it. One sees it in the lying and deceit. ("Thou shalt not bear false witness" was one of the "traditional moral values" championed by the Right until Oliver North and Elliott Abrams decided nine made a more fitting and flexible decalogue.) One sees it in their indifference to the human costs of ideology, and one sees it in their haste to make the law subservient to it. Historic conservatism as law at its core. Indeed, Walter Lippmann wrote that "the gradual encroachment of true law upon willfulness and caprice is the progress of liberty in human affairs." The belief that governments may not be arbitrary is, he said,

> the higher law, the spiritual essence without
> which the letter of the law is nothing but the for-
> mal trappings of vested rights or the ceremonial
> disguise of willfulness. Constitutional restraints
> and the Bill of Rights, the whole apparatus of due
> process of law in courts, in legislatures, among ex-
> ecutives, are but the rough approximations by
> which men have sought to exorcise the devil of
> arbitrariness in human relations. Among a people

which does not try to obey this higher law, no
constitution is worth the paper it is written on.

It is hard to maintain a constitutional order. We are asked to
be much more truthful, reasonable, just, and honorable than
the letter of the law. The government, too, must live up to this
exacting standard. The Constitution implies equality not only
in the protection by law of the least of us but in the demands
of its morality upon all of us, including those with the greatest
power. Lippmann again: "If the sovereign himself may not act
willfully, arbitrarily, by personal prerogative, then no one may
not. Majorities may not. Individuals may not. Crowds may not.
The national state may not."

Without that spirit, bad things happen. People get killed. Principles lose their force. Politics and policies fail. The worst excesses of the American experience have come in defiance of
this moral spirit — from slavery to lynching, from the Trail of
Tears to Wounded Knee, from the Palmer raids to Joseph
McCarthy's witch-hunts, from the rebellion of the Southern states
to the war in Vietnam.

Liberals too have made their own contribution to excesses
committed against the constitutional order — to the exaltation
of ends over means. When it came to Vietnam, two Democratic
administrations forgot that an excess of good intentions was
among the dangers against which the Founders erected barriers.
The reminder came expensively: hundreds of thousands of
casualties, 140 billion dollars, and a wrecked economy later,
liberal Democrats had not so much lost their capacity to govern
as destroyed it.

Opposition to the Vietnam War swelled eventually to an over-
whelming crescendo. Some people were against it because they
thought the war immoral. Others thought it unwinnable at an
acceptable cost. Most, I believe, came to oppose it because they

felt that the war lacked democratic legitimacy. It was not lawfully begotten; it had been started, enlarged, and continued arbitrarily. This is not ancient Athens, where the few thousand
free citizens could gather on the hillside to decide if the cause
were worthy of the sacrifice of human life; but the spirit of consent was violated during the Vietnam years, the contract
breached. Consent, the core of our political covenant, does not
come from the fine print of polls or even from an election, any
more than fidelity in marriage results from the ceremony itself. Consent is a moral act of commitment to a relationship
based on the reciprocity of trust. In an election a government
wins office only; it must win consent by continuing adherence
to democratic rule and practice.

The wartime example of England is illustrative. Even with the
nation under siege, Winston Churchill was painstakingly deliberate in explaining publicly the course of events and his choices.
It was vital to morale and victory, he believed, not only that
the people pass upon the decisions of government through their
elected representatives but that they take their share of the
responsibility.

A great testimony to the British endeavor came from an
American, Edward R. Murrow, who reported from London
through those dark and threatening years. When the war ended,
Murrow broadcast home a tribute to Britain's adherence under
stress to the principles and procedures of constitutional government. "The thing that impressed me most," he said,

> was not the demonstration of physical courage, . . .
> [not] Dunkirk, or the Battle of Britain. . . . The
> most important thing that happened in Britain
> was that this nation chose to win or lose the war
> under the established rules of parliamentary
> procedure. It feared Nazism but did not choose

> to imitate it. Mr. Churchill remained the servant
> in the House of Commons. The government was
> given dictatorial power, but it was used with
> restraint.

Murrow recounted that while London was being bombed in the daylight, the House of Commons devoted two days to discussing conditions under which enemy aliens were detained on the Isle of Man. "Though Britain fell," he said, "there were to be no concentration camps there." He recalled that two days after Italy declared war on England, an Italian citizen convicted of murder in England appealed successfully to the highest court in the land, and the original verdict was set aside. As Murrow witnessed, "Representative government, equality before the law, survived."

More recently, Corazon Aquino, the president of the Philippines, though her country is beset by troubles on every front, has warned the military that counterinsurgency must not entail lawlessness. "There is a strong temptation," she said, "in dealing both with terrorism and with guerrilla actions, for government forces to act outside the law. Not only is this morally wrong, but over a period it will create more practical difficulties for the government than it solves."

America's own experience demonstrates the practical advantages of keeping the bargain of democracy. The political scientist Walter Clemens, Jr., has written that the most successful achievements of U.S. foreign policy — the Marshall Plan, for one — have been planned and conducted openly, while the most disgraceful failures — the Bay of Pigs, Vietnam — were those whose essential details were kept from the public.

In this light, Clemens says, even the triumphs of that celebrated Machiavelli of modern diplomacy, Henry Kissinger, have to be reconsidered:

Kissinger managed to meet secretly with Vietnamese in Paris, fly secretly to Peking and launch
normalization with China, and negotiate the SALT I
arms pact through a "back channel" to Moscow.
He even managed to keep U.S. air attacks on Vietnamese in Cambodia from the American public
for some time. But most of these operations soon
backfired. Hanoi took over the south; Japan
suffered a deep shock from being left in the dark
about China; Moscow gained concessions through
the back channel that have shaken public support
for arms control; and Cambodia has been ruined.

Nor has the Reagan record had even the consolation of short-
term achievement. Clemens writes:

Whatever the Reagan public relations machine
says, the facts are humiliating: The Marines have
been driven from Lebanon; the International
Court has found the U.S. a lawbreaker in
Nicaragua; the State Department's spokesman
resigned over the White House disinformation
campaign against Libya and the public does not
believe the President when he claims that he did
not cave in to Moscow or Tehran to secure U.S.
hostages.

Why, Clemens asks, do truth and openness work best in peace-
time? "Because they minimize damage and maximize the
prospects for creating values for all sides. The more voices and
interests with access to necessary information can make themselves heard, the more likely that governments are to act wisely."
This point is reinforced by Gregory F. Treverton in his recent

book, *Covert Action: The Limits of Intervention in the Postwar World*. By their very nature, he argues, secret operations can be discussed only by a limited number of people, inviting the kind of intimacy that limits debate and criticism. "Whatever else may be said of the Bay of Pigs operation," he writes, "one of its key premises — that discontent in Cuba would quickly translate into open assistance for the invaders — was never believed by the CIA's intelligence analysts. Yet they never had a chance to register their dissent directly, for they never even knew of the plan."

When President Reagan began to run arms to Iran, the White House kept such tight control of the operation — cutting out of the discussions not only Congress but the Cabinet and the Joint Chiefs of Staff — that "it denied itself CIA and other assessments that undercut the premises of the operation." No one at the White House consulted those analysts scattered through the government who could have warned the president against believing that Ghorbanifar had leverage with the ayatollahs or that Iranian "moderates" existed who might be separated from the "radicals."

The president appeared shocked when the public responded with disgust to the trading of arms for hostages, as if the public should not have taken him at his word when he promised that he would never do business with terrorists. But the president might not have pursued the duplicity in the first place, Treverton says, if he had established a review process that could have set off warning signals: "The views of Cabinet officers, White House staff who attend to the president's interests, and Congressional overseers ought to be seen as surrogates for public reaction." Secrecy permitted the duplicity and stupidity to go unchallenged. America suffered costly and embarrassing setbacks in the world, and at home the pillars of our constitutional order were shaken.

So not for trivial reasons did the Framers fear the impenetrable concentration of arbitrary power in the hands of a few men tightly encircling a president. It is in secrecy that the bacilli of self-deception thrive unexamined, producing that peculiar Washington disease known as Potomac Fever, which causes one's head to swell and one's mind to shrink. Unless inoculated by facts and informed opinions — rare in the protected coterie of the like-minded — it can rage like an epidemic in the highest realm of government, with devastating costs to the democratic ideal. As the congressional report concludes, "Policies that are known can be subjected to the test of reason, and mistakes can be corrected after consultation with the Executive Branch itself. Policies that are secret become the preserve of the few, mistakes are perpetuated, and the public loses control of government."

What is secret is often squalid as well. In the dark, men were able to act contrary to the values they proclaimed in public. Paying lip service to democratic ends, they made league with scoundrels whose interest is anything but the survival of democracy. Arthur Schlesinger, Jr., once wrote that "the New Leftists believe in the omnipotence of the deed and the irrelevance of the goal." Today's New Right ideologues believe in the omnipotence of the goal and the irrelevance of the deed. So their tactics are those of the enemy they hate and fear, and they award America's franchises to con men, hustlers, terrorists, racketeers, murderers, and other sleazy characters who for a fee sign up in the crusade. Reading once again the Iran-contra report, I see the name "Ramon Medina." He is identified merely as an "associate" in the contra resupply operation — one of North's boys. His real name is Luis Posada Carriles, and I first came across his trail several years ago while working on a CBS documentary, "The CIA's Secret Army." He had been working in shady operations in Latin America. When terrorists blew up a Cuban jetliner in

1976, killing 73 passengers — many of them athletes — Posada was arrested and held by Venezuelan authorities. Reportedly he had helped mastermind the mass murder. After spending nine years in jail with no definitive resolution of the charges against him, Posada escaped. Now he has surfaced again, part of the network created by the Reagan White House to wage war against a government the United States recognizes.

José Bueso Rosa shows up in the congressional report too, although it is under the alias of "an official in a Central American country." The Honduran general had cooperated with the White House in setting up and supporting contra staging bases in his country. After Bueso was convicted of plotting to assassinate the Honduran president, North and other White House officials tried to get a pardon or a sentence reduction for him. Otherwise, North said, Bueso might "start singing songs nobody wants to hear."

Apparently no one was too unsavory for the cause. Not even Gen. Manuel Noriega, the strongman of Panama now under indictment by two U.S. grand juries for drug dealing and racketeering. So useful was Noriega to Colonel North and company that they ignored his penchant for running drugs, rigging elections, and murdering political opponents. According to Noriega's former confidant, José Blandon, among the services the general rendered the United States was military training for contra guerrillas at a time when the training was illegal. The United States apparently bought his favors with funds from the CIA. (Congress is only now following up allegations of drug connections to the private war in Central America. Ramon Milian Rodriguez, a convicted drug cartel accountant, has told a Senate Foreign Relations subcommittee that he funneled "millions of dollars" of laundered drug money to the contras through dummy companies — one of which received $250,000 in humanitarian aid [sic] from the State Department.)

In secret the road descends from fantasy to fanaticism, from moral relativism to moral hypocrisy. And the United States government becomes the ethical twin of the enemy. *His* rules become the rules of the game.

The zealots, alas, are unrepentant. The minority report of the congressional investigation dismissed the White House transgressions as "mistakes in judgment" and called for increasing both secrecy and the power of the president. One of the chief supporters and fund-raisers of the war against Nicaragua says the lesson of the Iran-contra scandal "is to be less public about what we are doing." A theoretician of low-intensity warfare, who has been a consultant to the Reagan administration, warns that the United States cannot successfully wage little wars around the world unless the media and Congress cooperate. The prescription is for more secrecy, not less, and there is a new rule for democracy: no debate, dissent, or scrutiny. The president would be able to deal with the Congress and the public like the poker player in Texas who told his opponent: "Now play the cards fairly, Jim. I know what I dealt you."

Can it happen again? The historian Walter LaFeber says it will: "If you can corrupt a system like this once, you can do it again and more carefully the next time."

There is fertile ground for it.

Spread out before me are letters from viewers who watched "The Secret Government." Some of them reveal just how close is the race between education and catastrophe.

"We think you were totally wrong in showing this to the people of the United States," says one high school student. "It is none of are [sic] business what go's [sic] on in foreign countries. We elected people to do that kind of stuff, and that's why they make big money."

And this: "I am appauled [sic] at the presentation. Who are

you to say our government is wrong? Why don't you try supporting it instead of undermining it? America, love it or leave it."

And: "I don't understand how you feel that uneducated farmers and housewives [those men and women interviewed at the end of the broadcast] could possibly concieve [sic] an accurate idea of what was going on. . . . You must understand that these people have no authority whatsoever. . . . The professor's opinion is a very stupid thing to believe. Did you know that most professors are communists?" (The FBI will find Professor Firmage practicing his subversion cleverly disguised as a deeply committed Mormon.)

But, happily, the mail ran in support of the broadcast by a margin of well over fifteen to one. Two themes were constants. First, every American ought to see it; many suggested it "should be part of every American child's history lessons." And second, "My God, what can I do about this?"

The answer seems obvious: educate ourselves about what the Constitution means and what the government is doing. But as Mrs. Lake, my piano teacher of forty years ago, knows, nobody will learn what he or she does not want to learn. When I read those letters from high school students horrified at the thought of questioning authority; when I am reminded by Benjamin Barber of Rutgers University that the real teachers of our seventeen-year-olds are "television, advertising, movies, politics and the celebrity domains they define"; when I read the lament of Mark Siebel (the foreign editor of the *Miami Herald*, one of the few mainstream news organizations aggressively to pursue the Iran-contra story) that editors "have been cowed into believing that they are somehow doing something wrong when they expose government wrongdoing"; and when I realize how narrow was the Iran-contra inquiry and that, of the five recommendations made in the minority report, four would increase secrecy in government, I am not optimistic that public education will happen soon enough, that the press will be vigilant, and that some of our government officials will ever learn the lessons of history.

Over my seventeen years in broadcast journalism, I have returned often to this subject because the issues are vital and because the principle of accountable power is now so repeatedly violated in the name of national security. I come to it, of course, with scar tissue from my own experience in government, and the urgency I feel is that of a member of Alcoholics Anonymous who sees the first telltale signs of addiction in a loved one. I see the presidency being destroyed and with it the public morality of which the president is the most conspicuous incarnation.

I did not think that Watergate would be the end of the story; too many voices made light of the matter, and the underlying effects of the system — a large White House staff operating in the sanctuary of presidential privilege — were left unchanged. Now I do not think the latest chapter in the story is the last one, either. The apparatus of secret power remains intact. The voices that airily dismissed Watergate now ridicule the "lessons" of Contragate and continue a spirited defense of lawbreaking, arguing that the United States cannot play by the rules in a world where others are lawless.

This cycle of rationalization and repetition is wasting the authority and economy of the presidency and the moral credibility of the nation. The more he and his staff choose to operate in the dark contrary to their publicly stated values, the more they fail. The more they fail, the more impotent becomes the presidency and the more inclined its occupant to hide his impotence behind cant, placebos, and pieties. Meanwhile, the public — that vast part of the public that no longer expects much from the political process anyway — grows more indifferent and cynical, while the highly vocal partisans, deluded by ideology and frustrated by democracy, scream for more of what has already led to unqualified disaster. Mark my word: there will be a sequel, and these two television essays will a decade hence reappear as part of a trilogy. This is not only unfortunate but unpleasant; it is far more pleasant as a journalist to visit poets, philosophers, and artists than to go rummaging once again among the debris of a failed presidency, finding in the litter bits and pieces of a shredded Constitution. But if poetry, philosophy, and art are to be around for our instruction and delight, not to mention the journalist's livelihood, first things must come first, most notably the preservation of our constitutional order. Freedom does have enemies in the world, but it has enemies at home too. Their menace increases in proportion to the shadows that surround them.

I do not mean to close this round as a pessimist. Skepticism is a good democratic virtue, but pessimism is the end of faith. I am optimistic in believing that ignorance can be cured. One starts by flunking the high school student who wrote me that "these people" — the "uneducated" farmers and housewives, and yes, the professors too — "have no authority whatsoever." The Constitution begins, "We, the People" because citizens *are* the source of authority in our country. This, I know, is a truism. But truisms are true, and Valerie Harrell — bless her heart — drilled this one into us back in tenth grade civics because she believed that democracy, unlike the Super Bowl, is no game and that citizens are not mere spectators. She knew that how we think about the Constitution is a measure of who we think we are. Do we disdain it, ignore it, shred it, obey it only when it seems convenient? Do we want to be a generous people, a fair people, an honorable people — most of all, a united and mutually respectful We-the-People? The Constitution is our covenant about these ideals, and there is no way to reach them if we discard the essential bond of the contract: none of us, not even the president, can pick or choose among the laws we wish to obey. A president who is nonchalant about this contract deserves to be impeached. A people who forget it will have invited the darkness. As a friend reminded me recently, "What you cannot see, can blind you."

BILL MOYERS has been in broadcast journalism since 1971. In 1986 he formed his own independent production company, Public Affairs Television, Inc., based at WNET in New York. Previously he was a CBS News correspondent, a senior news analyst for the CBS Evening News, and executive editor on documentaries for CBS Reports. For eight years before joining CBS, Moyers was executive editor of the highly acclaimed public television series, "Bill Moyers' Journal." He has received just about every prestigious award a broadcast journalist can receive, including ten Emmys, three George Foster Peabody Awards, the Alfred I. Dupont-Columbia University Award, the Sigma Delta Chi Award for Distinguished Service in Journalism, the George Polk Award for political reporting, and the Overseas Press Club Award for his news reports from Africa in 1985. His public television series, "A Walk Through the Twentieth Century with Bill Moyers," was named the outstanding informational series of 1984 by the Academy of Television Arts and Sciences, as was his 1981 series on creativity.

Deputy director of the Peace Corps under President Kennedy, Moyers also served President Johnson as special assistant and then as press secretary. On leaving politics he became publisher of Newsday, the Long Island newspaper, which during his tenure won 33 major journalism awards, including two Pulitzers.

A graduate of the University of Texas at Austin, Moyers received that university's Distinguished Alumnus Award in 1986.

For More About the Secret Government And Its Threat to the Constitution*

A Reading List

Adler, Mortimer J. *We Hold These Truths: Understanding the Ideas and Ideals of the Constitution.* New York: Macmillan, 1987.

Anderson, Scott, and John L. Anderson. *Inside the League.* New York: Dodd Mead, 1986.

Blum, W. *The CIA A Forgotten History.* United Kingdom: Zedd Press, 1986.

Colby, William, and Peter Forbath. *Honorable Men: My Life in the CIA.* New York: Simon and Schuster, 1978.

Commager, Henry Steele, ed. *Documents of American History,* 9th ed. Englewood Cliffs, N.J.: Prentice-Hall, 1974.

DeSilva, Peer. *Sub Rosa: The CIA and the Uses of Intelligence.* New York: Times Books, 1978.

Dickey, Christopher. *With the Contras: A Reporter in the Wilds of Nicaragua.* New York: Simon and Schuster, 1985.

Gaddis, John Lewis. *The United States and the Origins of the Cold War, 1941–1947.* New York: Columbia University Press, 1972.

Higgins, Trumbull. *The Perfect Failure: Kennedy, Eisenhower, and the CIA at the Bay of Pigs.* New York: W.W. Norton, 1987.

Hinckle, Warren, and William W. Turner. *The Fish Is Red: The Story of the Secret War Against Castro.* New York: Harper & Row, 1981.

Karnow, Stanley. *Vietnam: A History.* New York: Viking Press, 1983.

---

*All the books on this list can be found in local libraries. Most are still in print and available from their publishers.

Kwitny, Jonathan. *Endless Enemies: America's Worldwide War Against Its Own Best Interests*. New York: Penguin Books, 1986.

Marshall, J., P. Dale Scott, and J. Hunter. *Iran-Contra Connection: Secret Teams and Covert Operations in the Reagan Era*. Boston: South End Press, 1987.

McGehee, Ralph W. *Deadly Deceits: My 25 Years in the CIA*. New York: Sheridan Square Publications, 1983.

Mee, Charles L., Jr. *The Genius of the People*. New York: Harper & Row, 1987.

Padover, Saul K. *The Living U.S. Constitution*. New York: New American Library, 1969.

Ranelagh, John. *The Agency: The Rise and Decline of the CIA*. New York: Simon and Schuster, 1986.

Report of the Congressional Committees Investigating the Iran-Contra Affair, with Supplemental, Minority, and Additional Views, November 1987. Washington, D.C.: Government Printing Office, 1987.

Roosevelt, Kermit. *Countercoup: The Struggle for the Control of Iran*. New York: McGraw-Hill, 1981.

Schlesinger, Arthur M., Jr. *The Imperial Presidency*. New York: Popular Library, 1974.

Schlesinger, Stephen, and Stephen Kinger. *Bitter Fruit: The Untold Story of the American Coup in Guatemala*. New York: Doubleday, 1982.

Sick, Gary. *All Fall Down: America's Tragic Encounter with Iran*. New York: Random House, 1985.

Smith, Bradley F. *The Shadow Warriors: The OSS and the Origins of the CIA*. New York: Basic Books, 1983.

Taking the Stand: The Testimony of Colonel Oliver L. North. New York: Pocket Books, 1987.

Treverton, Gregory F. *Covert Action: The Limits of Intervention in the Postwar World*. New York: Basic Books, 1987.

U.S. Congress, Church Committee. Alleged Assassination Plots Involving Foreign Leaders. Interim Report of the Select Committee to Study Government Operations with Respect to Intelligence Activities. New York: Norton, 1976.

The Watergate Hearings: Break-in and Cover-Up. Proceedings of the Senate Select Committee on Presidential Campaign Activities as edited by the staff of The New York Times. New York: Bantam Books, 1973.

Woodward, Bob. *Veil: The Secret Wars of the CIA, 1981–1987.* New York: Simon and Schuster, 1987.

Index